MW00977282

Dixie Mobley

Two Gone, Too Soon

Dixie Mobley Short

PublishAmerica
Baltimore

First printing

PublishAmerica has allowed this work to remain exactly as the author intended, verbatim, without editorial input.

Hardcover 978-1-4560-2198-6
Softcover 978-1-4560-2199-3
PUBLISHED BY PUBLISHAMERICA, LLLP
www.publishamerica.com
Baltimore

Printed in the United States of America

Acknowledgements

To my son Donny Mobley, who had more patience than anyone I know while helping me with the computer work.

To my church, Loganville Baptist, for as a child that is where my faith began.

To my husband, Henry, who shared my grief.

To Nikki's mother Debbie, "I Can Only Imagine"

To all my friends, you know who you are.

To my siblings, Claud and Geneva Wilkerson, Catherine Wilkerson, Betty Wood, Connie and Bobby Knight, Patricia Wilkerson, and Ione Wilkerson, I send my love.

I dedicate this book to my children, Donny Mobley, Rick and Karen Mobley, Randy and Teri Mobley. Grandchildren: Nathaniel, Joshua, Aaron, Stephen, Michael, David, Hannah, Joseph, Elisabeth, Michaela and Josiah Mobley, Krista and Cassie Mobley with a love beyond words.

Foreword

By Donny Mobley

I grew up with what I suppose was the typical American dream: get married, buy a home, have kids, and grow old with a family. Little did I know that my dream would turn out to be a nightmare. If anything, my life turned out about the exact opposite as it could: unmarried, no kids, and no family; only growing old in solitude.

My life was typical of a teenager up through high school. I went to school, spent time with my girlfriend, and drank beer with my best friend. Life was good and I was looking forward to the freedom that so many others at my age revered. I was in love with my gal and dreamt of the future with expectations that all was good. We would buy a home, cook dinner together, make love, and have babies.

The first indication of impending disaster was after I joined the military. Having floundered for a year after graduation, I decided, or rather, my buddy and I decided while getting intoxicated at the local pub, that we would join the Air Force. Boot camp was my first venture away from home, from mom and girlfriend, and friends. It was the first time I had ever experienced home-sickness. I looked forward to mail-call until I received a dear-John letter from my girlfriend.

I never had given thought to unfaithfulness. The idea that a woman would cheat on her man was a concept so unfamiliar to me that the news that I was the recipient of such a letter shocked me to the core of my soul. At first there was disparity, followed shortly by anger. Then my upbringing and the lesson of forgiveness coupled with the unthinkable thoughts of being ripped out of a relation with my high school sweetheart took me to a place in my heart that was hard to embrace: bitter-sweetness.

No one should get married before the age of thirty, in my humble opinion. After returning from boot camp, I tried hard to understand the reasons explained to me just how someone whom I have developed a relationship could become promiscuous while I was away. I felt it was something I could forget and move on and so my high school sweetheart and I tied the knot. I was twenty; she was still a teenager. We were not prepared; nobody at that age is. However, I was stubborn and felt that by brute force I was going to fulfill my dream come hell or high water. What's a few bumps in the road, I asked myself. Let by gones be by gones; it is water under the bridge.

History is a murky soup and I have difficulty remembering precise details, but I do remember the emotions, the intense emotions that have its roots deeply embedded in my soul.

First, a surprise that a little bundle of joy is growing from my seed. The elation of knowing that one has created a new life is beyond words. I was to be a daddy; step one in the fulfillment of my dream is now complete. But the joy was quickly overshadowed by female hormones.

Pure hell; these are the words that any man would use to describe living with a pregnant woman whose own emotions rise and fall more quickly than a heartbeat. I found it hard to believe that someone could go from deep depression to raging insanity with no provocation. I seriously thought something wrong so I forced my wife to see a psychiatrist. Though they agreed that there was mental instability, she was obviously angered by the entire ordeal and became very vindictive.

At roughly six months pregnant, I get word from a friend of an event that disturbed me terribly, yet there was nothing in my power I could do to prevent it. Each Wednesday, one of the local pubs promoted "Tequela" night. I was horrified to hear that my pregnant wife was actually at the bar with her friends; and no, she was not drinking water, according to my source. One would think that the friends of a pregnant woman would intervene and discourage a pregnant woman from consuming alcohol, but apparently in their youth it was less a concern than having a good time.

Soon, Dana Nichole Mobley, was born. Despite the turmoil of the previous nine months, I was overjoyed at the birth of my daughter.

As I recall the months afterwards, my memory becomes more murky. I was working long hours on the military base and my wife was working evenings at a local hamburger joint. I would come home and care for Nikki while she cried nearly non-stop with colic. I didn't know what to do to make her stop and felt terrible that she may be suffering. I would lay on the floor with her until she fell asleep and her mother returned from work, which was early in the morning, much later than she got off from work.

I finally got tired of the late-night partying my wife enjoyed. Her careless attitude towards me pushed me to seek legal advice. The attorney suggested that I move out while the divorce proceeded. I did not see how that would help and the thought of leaving my daughter with her mother given her attitude was tearing at me. I wanted to just take Nikki and go; go anywhere. If it were not for being in the military I would have, but being AWOL was a serious charge, and I did not want to end up in a military prison, so I reluctantly decided to follow my attorney's advice, and attempt to get custody through the legal channels.

Weeks later, or maybe it was months, I cannot recall, I had a change of heart. I decided I could live with my wife and her partying ways, as long as I was able to be with my daughter and watch her grow up. Before the day I decided to go to my wife and ask to move back in, I spent a sleepless night wondering, worrying about Nikki.

Through all the murk, this one event is crystal clear in my mind. The sun had barely risen as I walked up to the door; I knocked and my wife answered the door. I explained to her I did not want to miss seeing Nikki grow up and I wanted to reconcile our differences. There was going to be no reconsideration in my wife's mind. Without pause, the answer was an immediate no. I begged and pleaded to no avail. When I finally gave up I was so full of despair I thought I was going to die. The only relief I was able to get was by turning that despair into utter hatred and anger. I was hellbent on getting sole custody and I immediately discussed this with my attorney.

Granted, my argument was weak. I knew I would make a better parent, a purely subjective notion, and the court obviously ruled in favor of the defendant. Again, I sank deeper into that hole called despair and I knew I would attempt to gain custody at a later time, but I would have to gather damning evidence if I were to succeed.

Having friends can be both a blessing and a curse. During a divorce they can be your eyes keeping tabs for you when you cannot. I would regularly get reports of my soon to be ex-wife's activities. Only just out of her teen years, she was taking full advantage of the freedom she never enjoyed, regardless of being a mother. She was a party-girl, often with baby in tow. One day I hear of an incident involving Nikki when, late at night at the hamburger joint, she was set atop a counter and left alone. Needless to say Nikki managed to fall off and land on her head.

It was like a nightmare from which one could not emerge. First came my old friend despair followed by its cousin anger. Then a new feeling introduced itself: Anxiety. I had to do something, and quickly, but I had no evidence, other than this incidence, and it in itself was not nearly enough to win a custody battle.

Soon, I began to hear rumors about her new boyfriend. It would be one thing if he was a hard-working man with similar aspirations as my own, but that was not even close to the case. He was a criminal, a petty thief, and God knows what else. And to make matters worse, my ex-wife had moved in with him.

It may be not enough evidence to win a custody battle, but I could not stand there and allow my daughter to be raised by a two-bit thief. I paid another visit to my attorney, who was all too willing to take my hard-earned money. I was hopeful that by the time my case goes to court I could find more evidence.

By this time I was working the graveyard shift. Not out of confidence but of hope, I rented a house. I wanted to do everything that would give me the best chance of winning custody, and living in an apartment would not cut it. With my mother's help, I set up Nikki's room. I couldn't wait for the first time she saw it.

I had difficulty sleeping while working the midnight shift. After twenty plus years of a typical sleep pattern, my brain was in revolt against me by trying to get rest at a time I would normally just be waking up. I asked my doctor for something to help me doze off and back in that day the prescribed medication was barbiturates. It would send me into a very deep sleep cycle and even after eight hours of sleep, I would still wake up groggy.

On a typical morning, I return from a shift and pop a pill just before crawling into bed. At some point, the phone rang and I was oblivious to whom was on the other end. Someone, or someone's dog had died, or so I thought. The caller was calling me to convey sympathies. I did not think twice about it until later, and just fell back into my slumber.

It could have been moments later or it could have been hours, I do not know, but I heard the front door open and my name being called by my girlfriend. She ran into the bedroom and embraced me and said, "Nikki is dead." Then I notice my mother and step-father there also. I assume that we hugged and tried to comfort each other, but I cannot precisely recall those memories.

It is difficult to describe the feeling of loosing someone whom you dearly love; emotional pain is so much different than physical pain, but it closely resembles having ones heart ripped out and the lungs collapsing in the void. There is an emptiness that was filled by the connection made by two individuals that is unable to be refilled.

To this day I still have no, or very little memory of the events that followed. At the funeral, I remember sitting on a couch as friends and family came by to convey sympathies, but nothing of the drive to Snellville or after the funeral. I remember sitting in court while the person responsible for my daughter's death was being sentenced. I returned to work, but I could not tell you when.

At some point throughout the whole ordeal, I learned how to avoid thinking about Nikki in an effort to subdue the pain. And as friends and family would mention her in passing, I learned to keep the thoughts at a distance. I feel guilty doing so but I did not have to deal with the emotions. I often pondered what I could have done differently to prevent Nikki's death but the events were out of my control and in the hands of another. I have come to accept that there may be a higher purpose beyond my understanding and pain and suffering is a part of life on earth.

Chapter One

If God had given me the choice of answering the phone on Sunday morning, February 8, 1981, and living with what I was about to hear, and how it would affect our lives forever — or stopping the world and letting me get off, I definitely would have taken the latter.

The phone rang early that morning, and I felt as though my heart had stopped beating for a moment. I knew something had to be wrong; the phone just never rang that early on Sunday. My husband, Henry, answered it. I heard him say "just a minute, I have got to break that to her gently". I drew in a knot. Is this the call I have been having premonitions of about Randy, my youngest son, being hurt in an accident? I had these premonitions twice, the phone would ring, and a nurse would tell me that Randy had been seriously hurt in an accident, and the hospital needed me immediately.

Henry turned to me and said, "Dixie, its Debbie. Nikki is dead." Nikki was my first Grandchild, and the little girl I had always wanted in my first Grandchild. I grabbed the phone and said, "Debbie, do you mean Betty is dead?" Debbie was my first son Donny's ex-wife and her mother Betty had cancer and had only a few days to live. "No, she said, Nikki died last night." I asked what in the world happened. She had her tonsils removed just three weeks prior to that, and I went down to stay in the hospital with her and take her to Donny's house and stay with her for the weekend to make sure she would be alright. I seemed to think only "MeMa" could take care of her after surgery. Debbie said, "I don't know, she died during the night." My only thoughts then were of Donny. Has anyone told him yet? She said they had not. Please do not let anyone go to him until I can get there. I have to be the one to tell him. I could not bear the thoughts of anyone else telling him his baby girl had died. I do not believe I could have made the trip to Warner Robins if I had known how she died.

I started crying and screaming. I just cannot believe this has happened. My middle son Rick got out of bed to see what was happening. He called his church to tell someone he would not be there that morning. I called my sister, Betty, to tell her Nikki had died. She called me back and said she and her husband, Donald, would drive us down to Warner Robins. Somehow, I managed to pack a few clothes to last us for several days and for the funeral that I expected to be there.

Before leaving, Norris Wilkerson, a cousin of mine from Rick's church who was the Associate Pastor called me and asked if there was anything he could do, and prayed with me. I thanked him, and not in my wildest imagination, would we be bringing her back to Snellville to bury her and need him to do her funeral. For the first time since I had moved from Warner Robins, I realized the need for a church and a Pastor. I had been very active in church down there, but after re-marrying, moving here, and building a new house, I just had not started back to church.

My youngest son, Randy, had moved into an apartment just a few days prior, and did not have a phone yet, and I did not know where the apartment was. I called his girlfriend and told her about Nikki and asked her to go tell him, and tell him we were going on to Warner Robins and for him to come on down. Just last night as I was hemming a pair of pants for Rick, the thought crossed my mind — "but Randy does not have a suit."

Betty and Donald arrived, and after notifying all the family, we left to start the trip to Warner Robins, which would take at least two hours.

In the car down, I could not help but think of the time I came down this road for the first time. It was Donny's 15th birthday, March 8, 1972. How good it seemed to be back in Georgia. The boy's father, Don, was in the Air Force, and we had been stationed in Newfoundland, Wyoming, and Virginia, and after such cold weather, that beautiful day in Georgia just seemed like it was opening up just for us and our lives would be beautiful and happy forever. Little did we know that what lay ahead for us in Warner Robins would be unbearable and ruin my life and Donny's forever.

Their father, the three boys, and I arrived in Warner Robins with our camper and lived in it for a few weeks until we could purchase a house.

The boys, Donny age 15, Rick age 13, and Randy age 11, all had a hard time adjusting to a new place. After all, we had been in Virginia for the past four and half years, and they had made some very good friends there. They just knew there would not be any friends like them anywhere else. The letters would come from their friends telling them how much they had cried for them. One girl wrote the day they left they all cried until they dehydrated. It was not too long though before they started making new friends. Mike Perry became Donny's first friend and we still keep in touch with him.

All will be well now. We are living only a hundred miles from our parents. We had not lived near them in many years. Things would just have to be wonderful here. Don had a heart attack while living in Virginia, and the Air Force told us they would send us anywhere we wanted to go for his medical retirement. I was in the hospital after just having surgery when he had the heart attack. When I recovered from surgery, and Don was able to travel, we chose Warner Robins, Georgia because it was the closest active base to our parents.

Settled in our house, the boys were adjusting and making many new friends, and I had met some nice people. My cousin and his family lived just two blocks away, and how smooth I thought things were going, but I was wrong.

Soon Don began to seem restless since he retired. The doctors had already told me to be prepared to work and take care of myself just in case he had another heart attack and did not live. I had not worked except for a part-time job while the boys were in school. I did not want anyone else enjoying the years of my sons growing up.

I did not feel I needed a career. We were retired military, and after spending twenty years with Don in the Air Force, I thought I would always have an income, even if he did not live. Being with my children was the most important thing to me. Then Don decided to leave us and make a life of his own. I knew exactly what he meant by enjoying his life as we had already had many, many fights about his drinking, frequenting the Clubs, and gambling constantly. I did not want to live this kind of life. After all, I had three children to care for.

After Don moving in and out of the house five times in less than two years, and on the advice of my doctor, my pastor, the five marriage counselors we had been to, and the Police, I divorced Don even though it was against everything I believed in, but his actions were becoming unbearable, and I often feared for my life. I could see Don was not acting like a normal person, and I discussed this with the Air Force doctors. I expressed to them that something appeared to be wrong with his mind. They said, it was probably the medication he was taking for his heart, and the best thing I could do was to divorce him.

Don moved to Atlanta and re-married. Donny decided to go in the Air Force after graduation, Rick went to College in Atlanta and stayed with his father during the week, and came home on the weekend. At 3 o'clock in the afternoon, I could look up from my desk at work and see his little orange car turning in.

With both the older boys away, and me being almost forty years old, I decided to go to Vocational School to refresh my skills. I realized I would be on my own now. I had always thought that I would have a retirement check from the Air Force, and had not worried about a career. Little did I know how that retirement check would not come to me, but go to someone else who did not put a day in the Air Force. I try not to be bitter over the fact that the years I spent with Don in the Air Force, moving all over the world with three small children, leaving my family, and the retirement check going to another wife that never experienced any of the hardship. How unfair life seems sometime. I decided not to dwell on that, although my children still get upset thinking about this. If God had meant for me to have it, things would have been different. He must have another plan for me.

After I finished my courses in school, I got a job with Real Estate Company as a bookkeeper.

What happened to my safe and secure family that I thought I had all the years? My family is going in so many directions. I felt so lost and lonely. I wanted my family back just as it had been when the boys came in every evening, and I knew they were safe in bed. Now one is in the Air Force, one away at College, and Randy and I are alone in Warner Robins.

At the Real Estate Company where I worked, I met my husband, Henry. He was a developer from Atlanta down there to develop a Subdivision at the company for whom I worked. After dating for almost a year, we married and moved to Snellville and built a new house. Except for leaving Donny in the Air Force stationed in Warner Robins, I could put my family back together again. Rick moved back in the house with Henry, Randy and me. Donny had a steady girlfriend, and I knew she would be there for him, and he would be happy, or so I thought. Donny and Debbie married the fall after we moved away.

I remember telling Debbie I sure would like to be a Grandmother. I was so happy when they called me and told me they were expecting a baby. I prayed it would be a girl. They let me help with naming her. There were two beautiful little girls living next door. One named Nicole and the other Tiffany. I wanted to name her Tiffany Nicole, but they wanted her first name to start with "D" as did their names, so Dana Nicole was to be her name. Her nickname was "Nikki."

Things did not go as well for them as I had hoped. Within a few months after Nikki was born, they divorced. Donny wanted so badly to have custody of Nikki. He felt he would have been the best parent for her. He filed for custody after hearing rumors that Nikki was not being cared for, but lost.

My heart ached. Would I get to see as much of her as I wanted to? So often after a divorce, the Grandparents lose touch with the children of a divorced couple. No, this would not happen in this case. Debbie would let me see Nikki; she knew how much I loved her.

I wondered what her Grandfather Don would have thought of her being dead. He would call me at work and talk to me about the children and Nikki, and made a statement if anyone ever hurt her, they would have to answer to him if it took every cent of money he had to see that she was safe.

One day Don called me at work and told me, he and his wife were having problems. He suggested that maybe we could get back together and asked me if I would meet him. I told him I may talk with him, but I knew in my heart that I could never go back with him under any circumstances. There had been too many hurts in our marriage.

I never got the chance to talk with him. One Saturday Rick had visited his father. He came home and told me that his dad acted very strange; he stumbled when he walked and his voice was slurred. I asked him if his dad had been drinking and he said he had not. After Rick told us of his actions, we thought perhaps he had a stroke.

A few days later, I received a call from his family telling me Don was in the hospital and they suspected he had a stroke.

It was just a few days later that we received the news that it was not a stroke, but in fact, he had a brain tumor and only had a very short time to live.

On Easter weekend, I went to Warner Robins, brought Nikki here, and took her to the hospital for him to see her. I took pictures of Don and Nikki for her to have when she grew up...I thought.

I felt when the boys were older, that maybe they would think that this tumor had been there during this terrible time we had with him, and maybe they could forgive their father for some of his wrongdoing. I am letting the boys assume it was the brain tumor that caused all my beatings, but I know in my heart that it was not. I hid as much of the torture as I possibly could from the children. The beatings started soon after we were married. Back then if you made your bed, you had to lie in it. There were no women's shelters to go to, and we were stationed in far off places like Newfoundland, Wyoming, and Virginia. I could not go back to my parents because they did not have room for three children, and me, plus could not afford us.

On one of Don's visits home from the hospital, someone from Grandmother Mobley's family called me and suggested that maybe all of us come to visit Don. I had stayed close with Mrs. Mobley as she was the children's Grandmother, and I loved her. We continued to have her with us for all the holidays and special occasions. I was at the hospital until the minute she passed away.

We called Donny and he drove up from Warner Robins and met Henry, myself, Rick and Randy at Don's cabin at the lake. Don's wife was very pleasant. I kept my distance knowing I was the ex-wife, and we stayed a short while and left.

The short time he had to live had come sooner that we thought. I received a call four weeks after learning of his brain tumor that Don's condition had worsened, and Rick and I went to the hospital. Henry stayed home to wait for Donny, as we had to get the Red Cross to request emergency leave for him. I went on with Rick. Randy told me he could not go, and he hoped I understood that he could not go and watch his father die. He was so young to be going through this.

We arrived at the hospital, and I knew that it would not be long before he would be gone. I did not know if Donny would get there in time or not. The doctor came in and asked me if I had notified all the children.

We took turns staying in the room with Don. He looked terrible, and I was glad Randy did not see him. My husband Henry took his turn staying with him. During my turn with Don, he kept trying to tell me something. At the same time, his sister-in-law, Helen, came into the room to relieve me. She could tell he was trying to tell me something, and she motioned for me not to let on she was there.

"Don, are you trying to tell me something about our boys"? He nodded his head, yes. I said, "Don, we have three very good boys, and I am going to take very good care of them." He nodded yes. Then he started saying in a very urgent tone of voice, "Let's go, lets go." I asked, "Don, where do you want to go"? "Let's go home, Dixie." He spoke those last words just before going into a coma and dying in just a few hours. This was May 22, 1979. I do not remember where his wife was during all this time.

As if things were not bad enough for me, just eleven months later on March 15, 1980, my father passed away suddenly. I had gone to have lunch with him and my mother on Friday and Daddy seemed in such a good mood. At the table, he started talking about Nikki, "that little doll," as he called her. He said he sure would like to see her. I thought, "I'll go get her tomorrow and surprise him." I called Debbie and she said I could come for her and keep her for a week.

Rick and I left out early Saturday morning for Warner Robins for Daddy's surprise. Henry had gone grocery shopping and Randy at his Saturday job. I did not tell anyone else where I was going because I really wanted it to be a surprise for Daddy.

Rick and I stopped by to get Grandmother Mobley to go with us. We arrived at Donny's and I left Mrs. Mobley and Rick there and went for Nikki. I packed her things in the car. I arrived back at Donny's to visit a while before heading back to surprise Daddy. When I got there Donny said, "Mom, Aunt Betty called and wants you to call her, that PaPa is very sick". I called Mother's house and asked Betty what hospital Daddy was taken to, and I would take Nikki back to Debbie's and go straight to the hospital. She said, "No, just come on by the house." I knew then that Daddy was dead. He did not wake up that Saturday morning. I thank God for taking Daddy the way he did. Daddy watched television on that Friday night, and seemed in good spirit and went to bed his usual time. He did not get up his usual time the next morning, and Mother went in to check on him and he had died peacefully in his sleep. I was sorry it took them so long to fine me and I will never go out of town again without telling someone.

I felt as though my world had stopped. Daddy was the first of our large family to die (except for the boy's father). The boy's father had just died eleven months earlier. I felt as though there was a huge hole, and I could not fill it up. I just felt so empty without Daddy.

I knew though that I had to keep my own family going. Losing their father and grandfather so close together was very hard on them. I would carry on; not knowing the third was yet to come in just a few months.

I had arranged with Debbie to let me keep Nikki for a week just before Thanksgiving. I called so many places, checking on nursery's for her for Monday, Tuesday, and Wednesday. I would be off Thursday and Friday.

I could not just leave her with anyone. I had to be sure she would be safe. I found a nursery just a few doors from my work and talked with them. They seemed to be fine and if she cried, I asked that they call me immediately. The first day she seemed a little hesitant to stay, but I felt sure they would come for me if she needed me.

The second day I was very embarrassed to take her to the nursery. Randy and his friend, Jud, took her into my bedroom and drew a smiling face around her "belly button" with my eyebrow pencils and lipstick. I could not get it off with regular washing, so rather than cause her to be uncomfortable with scrubbing, I would just explain to the nursery. They looked at her and burst out laughing.

On Wednesday, we were on our way to the Nursery. She had on a little blue coat that I had given her for her birthday. She was sitting in the seat beside me, (seat belts were not installed in cars then) and I was singing "Good Morning to You, Good Morning to You", and she was nodding her precious little head with me in time with the song when all of a sudden it was like a voice saying to me "Back off, you are loving her too much". It startled me so, I looked in the back of the car to be sue no one was in there with us. All of a sudden, I could not see a vision of Nikki. It was as if I was looking into the sky, and could not see her.

I knew it was God telling me something. What in the world are you trying to tell me? I had heard that Debbie might move to Florida with Ricky Pugh. Surely, that would not mean that I would not see her. There was nowhere on earth that she could move to that I could not drive, walk, or fly to see Nikki.

I was troubled all day at work. I kept seeing this blank space and could not put Nikki in it.

I enjoyed her Thanksgiving Day, and spent Friday enjoying her even more because I had the day off with her and did not

23

have anything to do but spend it with her. She enjoyed being here with me I could tell.

Rick wanted to put her bed into his room. When he would come in, I would tell him to be very quite that she had gone to sleep. A few minutes later, he would come in the living room with her in his arms say, "guess who woke up." She was usually in the bed with him in the mornings when I went in to check on her.

Every time I had Nikki at my house, I just could not let her out of my sight. Rick often wanted to take her to Sunday school with him. I guess you could call it selfish on my part, but I made excuses to him that he was not use to driving with a baby and may have an accident. He stated that they had such a good nursery at his church and wanted so much to take her. As far as I know, her precious little feet never entered the doors of a church. I am sure that she is in heaven though.

Chapter Two

Thanksgiving week was over, and I had the dreadful task of taking her home. When I took her home, I was standing in the doorway talking with Debbie, and looked back and she was back at my car trying to open the car door. How I hated to have to leave her.

When I went over to Donny's after leaving her with Debbie he said, "Mom, I am afraid I have some bad news." He had heard that Debbie was living with Pugh again. She had left him and moved back into the house with her parents, and Donny had dropped his second custody case, as we both knew Nikki was safe if she were with them. Donny said he would have to start lining his ducks up again and get enough money to file for custody again.

Even though Debbie was living with her parents, I had some serious concerns. Debbie had a younger brother, Davy, who also lived there. He had been in a lot of trouble, and I just could not put my finger on the problem, but I just did not trust him. Surely, Nikki would be all right with Debbie and her parents there, but I still worried.

I began to get more depressed over her, and continued crying more and more to move down to Warner Robins to be close to her. I started having premonitions about losing her. I even had planned that if she were kidnapped we could sell the house and use the money for ransom. Surely, we had enough equity in the house to cover it. I know now God was telling me something, but I did not understand what. Was it because I had wandered away from Him after coming up here and just got too busy to think about Him?

We discovered the reason Nikki was not talking was that she could not hear words clearly and would need to have tubes put into her ears to drain the fluid and have her tonsils removed. I suggested to Donny that he wait until that was over before filing for custody again. He was in the process of purchasing a home, so he could prove he had a good place for her.

In addition, we had heard the bad news that Betty, Debbie's Mother had cancer and had a short time to live. We cannot be in the middle of a custody suit when Betty dies. We will have to bide our time.

Debbie seemed to be having a hard time making ends meet, and I had heard that she had broken up with Ricky Pugh again. I visited her and asked her to come to Snellville and live with us. I told her she could go to College at night and I would keep Nikki, and she could live free with us until she could get more education, and get a job and enough money to move out on her on. She called me a few weeks later and told me that Pugh had gone to Florida, and if he did not come back that weekend, she would take me up on my offer. She had called Donny and asked him if he minded her living with us. I knew it would be hard for Donny having Debbie up here when he came to visit, but somehow I knew we could work that problem out, after all, Nikki's well being was the most important thing now.

TWO GONE, TOO SOON

Donny called me that weekend and told me that Ricky Pugh did in fact come back and Debbie would not be moving here with us, but he was coming home for a visit and bringing Nikki. Debbie had discovered that Nikki's eye was injured. She did not know how it happened. She thought she had hurt it in her crib. The doctor said it could have happened only from a blow to the head. Why the doctor did not question the incident more is still a puzzle to me. I questioned Debbie if she had left her at any time, and she had left her with Pugh to go to the store.

When Donny arrived with her, I became very upset after seeing her eye. It looked like a pool of blood. All you could see was red blood. I still feel guilty at times because I did not contact the doctor. We began hearing all kinds of rumors about her care, and Donny decided to file again for custody. He said he had wakened at night worrying about her and was crying.

All I could think about was Nikki. I had a feeling that I should move back to Warner Robins and see what was happening; seems like it was worse for me on Saturday nights. I would cry and beg Henry to move back to Warner Robins. He always refused. I considered moving back there without him, but Rick and Randy had set roots here. Would it be fair to move them again? They have all been through so much, or so I thought. This was nothing to compare to the future. In addition, I hated to leave my Mother without Daddy being there to take care of her. The torment continued...

I tried to remember the last time Nikki and Donny visited me in my home. It was during my Christmas get together with all my family. I had dressed her in a little red and white dress. Although she looked like a Princess in it, she did not like the dress on and I changed her into her "overalls." She had always acted like a tomboy. Of all the things she liked the most was a motorcycle. She called it "mo-mo." I remember feeding her before everyone else arrived, as I knew I would be busy and I had to make sure she had eaten. Although I watched her as she went to everyone and had a bite from his or her plate. Soon it was time for Donny to leave and to take her back to Warner Robins. The hospital scheduled her surgery and I would be going down in January to be with her.

Sure enough on January 19, I left work at 5 PM and drove to Macon to the hospital. When I arrived, I could hear her crying in the room before I went in. How it hurt to hear her cry, I could not stand the thought of her being in any pain. When I went in, I picked her up and she wrapped her legs around my waist and her arms around my neck. Debbie made a statement that Nikki knew she had it made now, and they could all go home. Donny had stayed with her the first night she was in the hospital.

She was very restless. I did whatever she wanted. When she wanted to sleep, she slept, when she wanted to be up, we were up. Around 2 AM, a nurse came in to check on her and we were sitting in the floor playing with a nurse doll someone had given her. The next day Debbie came to check her out of the hospital, and Nikki and I left for Donny's, where I would keep her until Sunday afternoon. The doctor said it would be safe for her to come up to my house in three weeks. If only I had a warning that day that it was to be the last I would hold her alive again.

I must stop day dreaming now. We are in the driveway of Donny's house and I must go in and do the hardest thing I will ever have to do in my entire life….or so I thought.

Chapter Three

After the long two-hour drive to Warner Robins, I do not know, yes, I do, God gave me the strength to go inside and tell Donny that his baby girl was dead.

I rang the doorbell and he came to the door and said "Mom, what is going on, Uncle Charles called and said you were on the way down and something about how sorry he was of someone's passing." Thank goodness, Donny had worked the midnight shift and was asleep when Charles called, and Charles had mispronounced Nikki's name, so Donny did not suspect he was talking about his baby. He thought Charles was telling him about another relative.

When I told him Debbie had called and Nikki had died, he put his head in his hands and cried. After a while, I called Debbie's mother to get the name of the funeral home and Debbie told me that Nikki was still at the morgue at the hospital. The word morgue sounded so cold. I felt chilled to the bone.

We left Henry and my brother-in-law Donald there with Donny. My sister Betty, Rick and I went to the hospital. We walked in and a man with a two-way radio met me. He asked who I was and I told him, and he took us into a room and asked where the mother and boyfriend were. I told him she had told me she was coming to the hospital soon. I began to sense something was wrong. Then they told me Nikki was murdered and they suspected the mother and boyfriend.

About that time, I heard Debbie scream and my son Rick looked down the hall and saw two police officers taking them away. They told me they had arrested Debbie and Ricky Pugh for Nikki's murder and Donny would have to come and claim the body.

I feel that I must have gone into a state of shock and disbelief. I knew at this time I was not going to tell Donny what had happened. I felt he would not be able to handle all of it at one time. I had to find a way to prepare him. He was only 24 years old, and too young to be going through this.

I told the men I was not going to tell Donny she was murdered, and asked if I could claim the body? They said I could, as they were probably not going to let Debbie out of jail for the funeral. I kept thinking about how Debbie had cared about Nikki, and I knew in my heart that she would not have had any part in the beating to death that the police officers had just described. However, I heard what the police officer was saying.

I was just so numb that all I wanted to do was get Nikki and Donny out of the town and just run home as fast as I could.

We somehow made it back to Donny's and I told him that they had arrested Debbie and Ricky Pugh for Nikki's death, and did he want to take her body to my hometown and bury her. He said he did.

We started arranging for her transportation to Lawrenceville. The funeral home embalmed her there in Warner Robins, and the hearse would follow us to the funeral home in my town. I did not understand why I could not wrap her in a blanket and hold her in the car, but they explained it was against the law.

I went into the funeral home in Warner Robins and asked the undertaker if I could see her. He told me I could, but not to unwrap her clothing.

I picked her up and held her. She felt like a rubber doll, and looked as though she was sleeping. She had on a pair of red pajamas with feet, zipped all the way up, still, I could see the bruises on her cheeks and neck, and one of her eyes did not look right. I do not feel I really understood just what had happened to her. I believe my world stopped turning that day.

On the way back, no one spoke often. Donny went back in the same car with us. Randy had come on down with his girlfriend. I looked back every few minutes to be sure the hearse was still behind us. I could picture the small body lying back there all alone and wished that I had ridden with her.

We arrived at the funeral home where I had made the arrangements and was met by the director at the door. They were extremely nice to us. I told them that I had seen her body, but my sister Betty had not and I would like her to see Nikki. They took us into the room with her.

I felt completely detached from my body. What is happening here? Why am I here? I noticed most of my family had already arrived at the funeral home, along with many other people. The thought had crossed my mind on the way that there probably would be just a few people at her funeral. That was the opposite. By dark, the funeral home was completely full. People were so nice.

Valerie Wages, one of the directors, arranged with Belk's Department Store for the manager to meet with Donny and me to choose a dress for her. The store had already closed. We choose a pink dress in which to bury her. We chose her a little white coffin, managed to make all the other arrangements, and it occurred to me that I had not called Debbie's parents to tell them where she is. All I wanted to do was keep on running away from the truth. Donny was still in shock, and I was giving him tranquilizers often.

When I called Debbie's parents, Debbie answered the phone. She asked why did we bring her up here and I explained what they told me that she would not be let out of jail, and we would have to claim the body, and I panicked and just wanted to get both Nikki and Donny out of town before he learned the truth. After I explained it all to her, she said she understood, but she would not come up for the funeral. The authorities released her on bond when she explained everything to them about Nikki's death, and they verified that she had been working that night. Debbie told me that she was not supposed to have worked that night, but had exchanged hours with a co-worker that wanted off.

She had left Nikki with Ricky Pugh around 4 PM on Saturday, February 7, 1981 to go to work. Debbie's sister was there around 5 PM and Nikki was fine. Ricky Pugh had wrapped Nikki in a blanket, placed her on the back seat of the car, and went for Debbie around 10 PM. Debbie did not take her out of the car as she was carrying a Pizza, so Pugh removed her from the car and placed her in the bed. Debbie said she later went into the bedroom to put her pajamas on and she seemed very limp, but thought it was because she was so sleepy. When she went in around 1 AM to check on her, she was stiff. She got in her car and ran for the nearest phone to call an ambulance. A woman followed her home and performed CPR on her but it was too late.

During the conversation with Debbie, I promised her that if she would come up for the funeral, I would see to it that no one would mistreat her. She had expressed concern that they would. I spoke with her mother, Betty. I promised her that I would take care of Debbie if she would come for the funeral. She told me she would think about it. I also promised her I would have a picture of Nikki taken in the coffin and send to her as she could not make the trip up here.

Chapter Four

On Monday, Donny and I left for the funeral home very early. We had to spend as much time with her as we could. When we got there, Donny combed her hair and asked if someone would get some barrettes for her hair. He later put them in her hair. She looked so precious lying there in the white coffin with a pink dress on.

A very dear friend and her daughter, Nita and Bonnie Holt called me and asked if there was anything on earth that they could do for us. I told her I would like a small Bible to place on her pillow and would like to have printed on front "Go with God." Nita and Bonnie found a precious little pink Bible that looked so special with her pink dress. I wrote her a special message inside. I cannot thank them enough for getting the Bible. Nita, Bonnie, and Joe have been wonderful friends of ours since the early '60's, as we were all stationed in Newfoundland. We kept in touch with each other and finally they moved to Snellville, Georgia near us. I do not know what I would have done without their support.

Donny asked me if he could put anything in the coffin with her. I told him he could put anything he wanted in there. He sent back to Warner Robins for her book she enjoyed him reading to her. He placed it in her hands and she looked as if she was lying there reading it. Then he asked if he could put a flower in her hand, as the word "flower" was one of the few words that she had spoken clearly. He chose a piece of an azalea that had just come in.

The flowers were beautiful. Rick and Randy had an arrangement in shape of a Bible. Some were of little animals in shapes of teddy bears and lambs. So many people came and friends that I had not seen for a very long time came and offered their help and sympathy.

On Monday night, so many people from Warner Robins began coming in. Randy came to me and said, "Mom, you had better tell Donny what happened, because people are coming in from Warner Robins, and they have newspapers with them, and it is on the front page." I do not know when I thought I would have to tell him, but he looked so helpless and so very, very young to be going through the death of his baby. I thought as long as he did not know, perhaps he would not hurt so much.

I did not have a pastor there with me at the time, my cousin was going to do the eulogy, but would have to come on Tuesday prior to the funeral as his father was very ill and not expected to live.

How lost I felt! My brother Louie's pastor was there and I had met him several times in the past, and he offered to assist us in any way possible. Thank God for Rev. Horace Parr. He went with Donny and I into a room at the funeral home and I had to tell Donny what happened to Nikki. He cried and said, "God, how she must have suffered". I suppose it was a good thing that neither of us knew the exact way it happened at the time. One can take only so much pain.

Debbie, her father, sister and a friend arrived at the funeral home on Tuesday morning prior to the funeral. Debbie went up to the coffin and got extremely upset because she did not have anything in the coffin from her. I took her by the hand and we went next door to a florist and purchased three roses, red, white, and yellow, one from Debbie's mother, one from her, one from Debbie's grandmother. She then pulled up a chair and sat by the coffin.

The two little girls from next door put a beautiful pink cross in the coffin with her.

When it came time for Tommy Wages, the Funeral Director, to take her body from her room into the Chapel for the funeral, (I noticed tears running down his cheeks) so many people told me I should keep the little pink Bible I had placed on her pillow. I became very confused as what to do. I asked Donny what I should do and he said, "Mom, let her have it." I lined all the family up one by one to kiss her good-bye. I felt numb. I went through all the motions, made it through the funeral without falling apart. That came later.

Sang at the funeral was a beautiful song, "Jesus has taken a beautiful bud, Out of our garden of love," how true were the words of that song. Taken from us was indeed a beautiful bud and never to be replaced.

It was a cold and rainy day. I remember at the cemetery someone handed me a heavy coat and I placed it over Debbie and my legs.

After the burial, all the family went to my house, which was just a couple of blocks away, to have lunch. Debbie and her family went also. I had offered to pay for an ambulance to bring Debbie's mother, Betty, up but she was not able to make the trip. I did have a photographer take pictures of her in the coffin for her to see.

Several women from the Real Estate Office where I had worked came over and served lunch to everyone.

While everyone was at my house, Donny and I had gone into my bedroom to talk, and it thundered so hard that it shook the house. Donny said, "Mom, God is angry."

We finally made it through the day, and everyone left to go home. Donny and I went back to the cemetery.

The next day, we got a call from the District Attorney that he would like to talk with us, so Donny and I decided to go back to Warner Robins and try to pick up the pieces. I do not know how I managed to drive there. All I remember of the trip back was it had just turned dark and a dog ran into my path and I hit it and became very upset.

Someone from the crime department had called and asked me if I would send them the red pajamas she was wearing at the time of her death. They wanted to run some tests on them. They promised me they would return them.

During this time, all the murders of Atlanta children were taking place. They told me they were just so busy with all that investigation, it would just take time to get them back to me. I never did receive them back, although I would have loved to have the last thing she had been wearing.

When we walked into Donny's house, Nikki's ghost was so strong. It was as if we could reach out and touch her. I believe we both felt it equally as strong, because we slept on the sectional sofa that night, as neither of us could go into her room. Friends had offered to have everything packed before we returned, but I felt it would have been too much a shock for him to go into her empty room, so they left it for us to do.

Donny had called me recently and was so excited. He had Nikki for the day and had purchased a bedspread and curtains for her bedroom. They were the very popular Strawberry

Shortcake design. He had made her bed and hung the curtains, but could not figure for what the two long things that remained were. I told him they the tiebacks for the curtains. He had spent a lot of time reading to her he said.

We spent the next few days talking with the police, trying to put the pieces together. Donny's friends began coming over and I decided it would be safe to leave him and go home. Just before I left, we went into Nikki's room, packed up her things, and loaded them in my car to bring home and store for him. I had to get back to go see Nikki at the cemetery. It was still so cold and rainy. I wanted to take a blanket there and cover her grave up. My son Rick kept telling me she was not there, she was in Heaven. I kept dreaming about her night after night and would wake up so upset. One night in a dream, she was trying to crawl out of her grave and in my dream, God made me push her back. I guess that was his way of telling me she was to stay with Him. The dreams did let up somewhat after that.

The next few days and weeks were torture. I wanted to die also so I could go take care of her. After a while, everyone else has to go on living their lives, but you are still feeling the pain and grief.

Twelve days after Nikki's death, Debbie called me to tell me her mother had passed away.

We had been expecting this before Nikki's death. I was very sorry that Debbie and her family had to go through another funeral so soon.

I went down to Warner Robins to visit the family and to express my sympathy. The pastor of their church was there and he came to me and said he wanted to thank me for being so kind to Debbie and her family during Nikki's funeral. I cannot imagine anyone being any other way during a time like that.

I think I sat in the same chair day after day for weeks, and then I started praying. I had chosen the bay window in my bedroom to kneel and pray. I prayed that God would give me the strength to get through this, and he would give Donny strength, and look after Debbie. One morning in particular, I prayed to God to please give me some answers, or lead me to someone who could help me. I had not been back to "my chair" ten minutes when the phone rang.

It was Rose McKeever, a friend and the mother of my son Rick's friend. She asked how I was feeling, and I explained to her that I had prayed so hard for strength and answers. She said she had wanted to tell me something, and had asked Rick if he thought I was up to hearing what she wanted to tell me.

Rose had been attending a Bible Study Class at a church in Mountain Park. The teacher was Dawn Johnson, the Minister of Music's wife. Dawn had experienced something concerning Donny and me, and she asked if she could bring Dawn to my house. I could hardly wait for them to get there. I did not know what was going to take place, but I was reaching for any help I could get.

When they arrived, Dawn explained to me that in November, around the same day the voice spoke to me on my way to the Nursery telling me to back off, that I loved Nikki too much, that a voice had spoken to her also. She had written in her Bible, which she had brought, that she was to pray for Donny. When she went to the Bible Study Class, they said she would cry and ask everyone to pray for Donny. This happened up until the day of Nikki's burial. She said she did not know what was going to happen to Donny, but she knew that it concerned a baby. A few weeks prior to Nikki's death, she explained that the voice also told her to pray for someone named "Dixie." She said she did not know anyone named Donny or Dixie, but she was very distraught over all of it. On a cold and rainy Tuesday during the time we were at the cemetery, Dawn said she was in bed ill and the voice told her if she would go to 500 Memorial Drive, she would get her answer about Donny. She got out of bed and took a book and wrote inside "to Donny, if you need help, please call me," and signed her name and phone number. She drove in the rain to Memorial Drive and could not find the number 500. She saw a mail carrier and asked him where 500 Memorial Drive was, and he pointed across the street. It was a cemetery.

She was upset and confused as she felt she would not know what happened. The next morning as she was going again for the Wednesday Bible Study, Rose, who had not attended during this time Dawn was crying and asking everyone to pray for Donny and Dixie, met Dawn outside. Dawn asked Rose how her weekend had been and she said her friend Dixie's son, Donny's baby was murdered. Dawn said, "Donny and Dixie," and she knew this was her answer.

The next few weeks, Dawn became a very important part of my life. She came over often and prayed with me, and gave me a tremendous amount of strength. I attended several of her Bible study meetings. Everyone at the Bible Study said that all of this actually did take place.

I was trying to pick up the pieces and get on with my life. I decided to go back to my sisters and finish the wallpapering I had started before Nikki's death, and had not been able to finish until now. One of the days I was there, Randy called me and asked if I would co-sign at the bank for him to purchase a motorcycle. I got extremely upset and told him I would not. He said, "Mom, I'll be careful." I told him I felt he would, but I did not know about everyone else on the road. We had a terrible argument. I did not sign for the motorcycle, and we had not been on good terms.

Still, we have to go on. I was determined with God's help that I was going to make it through this crisis, but soon the rug was pulled out from under me again.

Chapter Five

In Memory of Nicole Mobley

God called little Nicole Mobley home
To Heaven the little darling has gone.
With tears in my eyes I cried, Oh! God, tell me why
As little Nicole in the grave will lie.

God has a plan for us all
Moreover, the time had come for little Nicole to answer his call.
So then as you lay her to rest
We thank God that he knows best.

We must never question his ways
Let us just be ready to meet her someday.
Dixie, this sorrow you will have to face
We only ask God to soften it with his grace.

May God lift your spirits high
Even though little Nicole had to die.
I know you will meet the test

As sure as the sun sets in the West.

For strong you'll have to be
As you ride life's waves as on the sea.
We know you will do what has to be done

Because you loved the dear little one.

To my dear friend Dixie in her time of sorrow!

Edna Spier.

So many people did such wonderful things for me. I had not realized how much people cared during a time like this.

An article in the Newspaper from Ken Dunlop reads:

Nikki Found No Help — Forgive me, Nikki, for not coming to your funeral. Seeing you in the casket was all I could take.

You looked like any 2-year-old girl asleep, but we knew you had died terrified, beaten until internal organs had ruptured painfully, beaten by an adult who loomed over you in a godlike rage, with win-milling arms that would not stop as long as you lived.

A sad-voiced cop in Warner Robins said they have someone in custody, charged with murder. But it's not for this sinner to judge him; mistakes have been made before. It was not as a judge, but as a parent with shaky credentials that I looked in your casket, Nikki, saw my own child, and fled.

Here in the office the quips we usually make about death, our feeble way of keeping human tragedy in perspective, were missing. People with kids of their own just shook their heads and asked, over and over, how could someone...

No one could answer that. Even Audrey Rogers, a counselor at Parents Anonymous, could not. She did know that the roots of child abuse often go back for several generations. You may have died, Nikki, because a 19th century sharecropper was a bad parent.

Those of us with children — children who are inarticulate, helpless, and sometimes cry unreasonable — wonder if we have it in us to do this. Was a great-great grandparent too free with his belt? Did a mother in the old country neglect her children, one of our ancestors?

If we do find ourselves abusing our kids, there is help. Parents Anonymous does not pass judgment. The people there just listen to parents who fear they may be going too far.

Neither you, Nikki, nor your killer found anyone to turn to for help.

I do not know who sent me this article, but I found it with all the other articles I had kept from the newspaper clippings. It had his picture in it and he looked so caring.

Chapter Six

In the Family Section of the Warner Robins paper, was an article about Donny. It shows a picture of Donny holding a picture of Nikki. Underneath the picture reads **"Donny Mobley holds photo of daughter, Dana Nichole, who died recently of severe internal injuries"** and underneath that was in large letters

"Father Lost Custody, Daughter Lost Life'.
The article reads:

Donny and his 2-year-old daughter spent Feb. 4 playing together, talking, and reading stories. It was one of the few occasions each month father and daughter had a chance to be together because of limited visitation rights granted in Mobley's divorce as well as his job responsibilities. "We always made the most of our time together, " Mobley said. "I always enjoyed having Nikki with me".

Four days later, relatives contacted the 23-year-old father and told him his only child, Dana Nichole Mobley, was dead.

"I couldn't believe it, I just couldn't accept it when I was told Nikki had died," Mobley said recently. "I still find it hard to believe".

According to reports from the Warner Robins Police Department, her mother, Debra W. Mobley, in their North Fifty Street apartment about 1 AM on Feb. 8th, discovered the toddler's body. Nikki, who was lying in a bed in the southwest bedroom, was taken to the Warner Robins-Houston County Hospital where she was pronounced dead on arrival.

An autopsy performed later that day revealed that she died of severe internal injuries, according to Houston County Coroner Daniel Galpin.

Police arrested John Ricky Pugh, who also lived at the Fifty Street residence, and charged him with the child's murder. During a commitment Hearing Feb. 20th before Justice of the Peace Nick Lazarous, the murder charge against 27 year-old Pugh was reduced to voluntary manslaughter, and the man was placed on a $25,000 bond.

Lazarous said he reduced the charge because no evidence was presented to "even imply that the death of the child was deliberate or intentional."

Police Detective Timothy McGee testified at the hearing that there were "about 15 to 20 bruise marks on the child's body."

It's hard to believe something like this could happen," he said. "When I last had

Nikki she was in good condition, feeling fine except for a cold. Last month she had her adenoids and tonsils removed at the Coliseum Park Hospital in Macon, and she was still recovering from that."

As for his daughter's condition at the time of her death, Mobley said he "never really had any reason to believe Nikki was being mistreated."

Despite the circumstances surrounding the child's death, Mobley said he harbors no ill feelings toward his ex-wife, who had custody of the youngster since their divorce in 1979. "I'm sure she and her family have suffered as much as we have since this happened," he said.

Twice since their divorce, Mobley sought custody of his daughter, but the attempts were unsuccessful.

"When I filed for divorce, I was going to ask for custody of Nikki, buy my lawyer said the chances were slim', he said. 'I was granted visitation rights every other weekend, and I got Nikki two weeks out of the year".

Mobley said he started court action to gain legal custody of his daughter in September 1979. In his petition, filed in Houston County Superior Court, Mobley claimed his ex-wife "through her neglect, carelessness, and negligence" permitted the child to "become repeatedly injured and hurt."

In her answer to the petition, Mrs. Mobley denied the allegations. Mrs. Mobley could not be reached for comment.

"We were in the courtroom for 15 minutes before (Houston County Superior Court) Judge Hal Bell threw the case out for lack of evidence", Mobley recalled.

Attempts to reach Bell for comment were unsuccessful.

Mobley aborted his second quest for custody in September 1980 when he realized he had no solid evidence to back his claims.

"My plans were to seek custody again," Mobley said. "I had been living in an apartment, but recently I bought a house so that I could offer a better home environment for Nikki when I asked for custody. I was waiting until I could begin working the day shift instead of the night shift at my present job before proceeding with legal action."

Again, Mobley said he had predicted a difficult battle in his continuing attempts to win custody of Nikki. "In order for me, the father, to get child custody I would have had to prove my ex-wife was an unfit parent," he said. "From my past experiences trying to get Nikki, it seems the courts still are leaning toward the mother."

"I think the courts have got to change and look at both the mother's and father's sides more deeply. I really believe a father can be just as good a parent as the mother can. I know I could have been a good parent to Nikki. I was financially able to take care of her and provide for her needs."

Georgia law says the mother and father have equal rights in child custody, said local attorney Robert L. Hartley, "but practically speaking, the wife gets custody 95 percent of the time unless both parents agree otherwise."

Warner Robins attorney Gene Harrington agreed that more fathers now are seeking custody of their children, but winning their custody is not so easy.

"When a father seeks custody of his minor children, he faces an uphill fight," Harrington said. 'Although more fathers are seeking custody than ever before, the deck remains stacked against them".

According to Houston County Superior Court Judge Willis B. Hunt, Jr., in most divorce cases the father generally agrees for the mother to have custody of their minor children.

"In only about one out of every 100 divorce cases is custody an issue," Hunt said. "Ordinarily when a minor child is involved, the parents reach an agreement concerning custody. The father generally does not seek custody unless the child is abused or neglected by the mother."

The father then must produce evidence proving his allegations against the mother, Hunt said.

The primary attitude is that if the mother is not unfit she should have custody of a small child, Hunt said. "But attitudes in that respect are changing. The courts are now willing to critique both parents in the situation. The courts primarily are looking for the best interest for the child."

Lazarous said he reduced the charge because no evidence was presented to "even imply that the death of the child was deliberate or intentional."

Now where in the world he could come up with that statement is beyond me. Did he think the baby could have beaten herself to death? The autopsy performed the day she was found stated she died of severe internal injuries. How could he account for all the bruises all over her little body? Once again, I am thinking someone is covering up something.

**The Daily Sun Received
Honors At GPA Newspaper Contest**
reading:

Rene Penn, A Daily Sun staff writer, won an award in the area of feature writing with a story that prompted this comment from the judges: "Father Lost Custody, Daughter Lost Life" - A moving story of a divorced father's reaction to the death of his child — sensitive, low-keyed but well done."

Chapter Seven

I had gone to bed early on Saturday night just before Mother's day and around 11:30; Rick came to my room and called to me. "Mom, he said, there is a lady on the phone from a hospital that says she must talk with you."

I ran into the living room and knew exactly what to expect. The woman repeated what I had the two premonitions about before Nikki's death. Randy had been seriously hurt in an accident and the hospital needed me there immediately.

It was May 7, Saturday night, around 11 pm; this was exactly three months to the day, night, and hour that Nikki died.

God, please do not let me lose another child! It is too soon. I do not believe I could survive the loss just now, but I came very, very close. Little did I know that would happen later?

When we got to the hospital Randy was critically hurt indeed. He had been riding on the back of a motorcycle with a friend when two young men in a car crossed the centerline and hit the motorcycle, almost tearing Randy's leg off. With Randy riding on the back of the motorcycle, his legs stuck out on each side. The car hit his left leg. The two people got out of their car and must have thought Randy was dead, because they jumped back in their car and sped away.

Thankfully, a car was coming up on the scene of the accident and saw the car running away, looked back and saw another car coming and hoped they would stop to check on Randy and his friend, and they ran after the car and got their tag number.

Randy was seriously hurt. A bone was sticking out from his upper leg, and most of his lower leg torn away. The paramedic told me later at the hospital that she had no idea she would get him to the hospital in time, as he had no pulse. Most of his blood had drained out. She said she kept telling the ambulance driver to go faster, and he told her he was going as fast as possible.

As soon as we got the call that night, Henry and I left for the hospital. Thank goodness there was not much traffic that time of the night as we went as fast as we could. I kept hoping a police would stop us and he could escort us on to the hospital as the call from the hospital told me to get there as fast as I could.

When I got there, I could see how serious it was. They said they were going to have to amputate his leg. He begged them not to, and I told them to do everything they could, as I had good insurance. We had the insurance from the Air Force, as well as insurance from Henry's work.

After the initial surgery that night, they put him in a room. Only the Chaplin and I could go in his room. It hurt him just to hear voices in the room. We could not to even touch his sheet. This was the same time a Turkish sniper shot the Pope. Later when we could talk in his room, and he could hear us, he looked up once when he heard about the Pope and said, "Who in the world would want to kill the Pope."

After about two weeks, they transferred him to Emory Hospital. There they started a series of surgeries. First, they drilled 15 holes all through his leg from one side to the other to put in steel pins to hold the leg together. His leg looked like tinker toys. He was in terrible pain. I stayed at the hospital with him, only to go home to take a shower and change clothes every few days. Most of the nurses were afraid to touch his leg, so I had to do a lot for him.

He had eight surgeries during the year. After several surgeries, they decided they should let him rest for a while and they allowed me to take him home for one month. They set his room up with the hospital bed and all the equipment he needed.

When I called the ambulance to take him back to the hospital, they had made a mistake and could not do another surgery for a few days, and told me I would have to take him back home until then. I told them I had used my last $100 for the ambulance, so they packed my car with pillows and blankets to make it like a bed for me to take him home.

My brother in California had sent me some money to help me out. I had purchased an old station wagon in which to transport him. When I got home, I had a terrible time getting him out of the car and into the house. He could not bend. I think a neighbor came over and helped me.

During this time he was home, many of his friends came over to see him. I had to have a breast biopsy during this time he was home and was in the living room resting, and one of his friends came through the living room where I was sitting, stumbling, and heading out for their car. I went into Randy's room and asked why they brought someone drunk over to see Randy. They said, "Mrs. Mobley, as his friends called me, he is not drunk, he passed out when he saw Randy's leg. I went out to his car and took him some ice water.

Many of our friends could not look at his leg. When one of my friends came to see him, I had to cover the leg with a sheet. Not many people offered to help me with him as his leg looked too horrible. In fact, the whole year he spent most of it in the hospital, no one offered to relieve me and stay with him. I guess I could not blame them though. It looked so horrible.

During the time I had the breast biopsy, just before they were to take me to the operating room, a nurse said to me, "my name is Nicole and I will be taking care of you." I did not have time to respond as I went "out." After the surgery, the doctor told my husband that he did not know what happened to me. He said I started crying and talking "something about a baby." I think just hearing the name Nicole upset me and started me to thinking.

Back in the hospital, the surgeries for Randy went on for a year. When he came home, he had to wear a special shoe with a brace that attached above the knee. He called it an "old man's shoe."

They asked him if he would donate the device where they had drilled the 15 holes through his leg to Grady Hospital as the doctor said so often they get someone that needed it. It was a very expensive device called a "Hoffman Device."

Dr. Fleeming was his doctor at Emory. Each time they did surgery, they took pictures of his leg for a book, as they had not before had a leg that badly torn up. The doctors would tell me he would never walk again and Randy told them he would. They would just look at me and shake their heads.

All the leg between his knee and ankle was missing, so there was no bone, no muscle, no anything. Just a fatty part of his leg was remaining in back. They took bone from his hip and put in his leg, and put in a Zimmerman stimulator. That made the bone grow and attach. They said they still did not think he could ever walk on the leg, as he would not be able to control his foot. He still maintained he would.

After the hospital dismissed him and he came home, I fixed him a room in the basement and his friend, Jud, stayed with him occasionally to keep him company. Down there he had been practicing walking without crutches and I did not know this.

I had to get a part-time job, as money was so tight. I got a job with Real Estate Company close to home. The broker let me go home ever few hours to take care of him.

When we went back to Emory in a cold January day, eight doctors came to evaluate him. They all sat in a circle in a room. He said to Dr. Fleeming, "I can walk without this shoe." Dr. Fleeming told him he would never be able to walk without that shoe. He kept telling them he could, and they told him "ok, let's see you." He pulled off the shoe and walked across the room.

All their mouths flew open in disbelief. Dr. Fleeming told Randy, "you need to get on your knees everyday for the rest of your life and thank God, number one for your life because you came so close to dying, and we don't know how you are doing it." It was truly a miracle. He never put the shoe back on. We walked out of the hospital in freezing weather with just a sock on. He took the shoe home and burned it.

His leg was one and one half inches shorter than the right one. I had to have all his shoes built up so he could walk better. Later on, a few years later he decided to have his other leg shorten to match the injured one.

His badly scarred leg is now a constant reminder. He was in Florida one time and the little kids asked him what happened to his leg. He jokingly told them, "Oh, a shark bit me over where you were playing."

He does well with the injured leg. He has a small limp, but handles it very well. In fact, he had a picture of a shark tattoo put on his leg.

I had tried a couple of times to talk with the police as to what the charges were against the driver of the car and I was treated as though I was the guilty one. Naturally, the car belonged to the boys' aunt and very little insurance. I was so glad that Randy could walk and did not pursue anything else.

Chapter Eight

While driving down the road one day I heard some awful news on the radio. They were talking about a man killing a woman in Macon, and slashing two of her children's throats who were twins and only two years old.

Then I heard the man's name and I almost ran off the road. It was Davey Whitten, Debbie's brother.

"Oh my God!" I exclaimed. I had always been afraid of leaving Nikki at the house of Debbie's parents because of Davey, but I though sure, since Debbie's parents were there, nothing could happen to Nikki.

Davey brutally stabbed 24-year-old Jana Lee Cole to death 26 times and he slashed her throat.

Another child was in the bedroom when his mother asked if anyone wanted something to drink. His little brothers said they did, and they went with their mother into the kitchen. The older child said he remembered hearing screaming and went into the kitchen. He then felt a man grab him from behind and felt a sharp pain on his neck. That was when he saw his mother lying on the floor and his brothers up against the wall with their throats cut too.

Then he saw the killer, David Alan Whitten, climbing out a window. The authorities arrested Whitten the following morning, hours after a neighbor discovered the children and mother's body.

Whitten told the judge who sentenced him that he broke into Cole's home to steal money to buy a new hunting bow. He did not mean to stab the mother or her children.

He told police the mother was asleep on a sofa when he broke in through a window, according to a police report. When she awoke, Whitten said he chased her through the house with a knife. Then he saw the children. "I turned around and saw them and cut their throats," he said. After I cut them, they were crying.

Whitten is serving a life sentence at Valdosta State Prison with out any chance of parole.

(I am writing this because of the end of this story.)

Chapter Nine

Every day I kept thinking I would hear that Pugh's trial was coming up, but nothing. I kept hearing things that Pugh was doing and became very worried that he would leave the country and I may not ever know what happened that I was hoping would come out in the trial.

Friends mailed Newspaper clippings to me from Warner Robins. I have a huge box of all the newspaper clippings I received.

Grand Jury Hands Down
Murder Indictments for three

John Ricky Pugh of Warner Robins was indicted for the Feb. 7 murder of 2- year old Dana Nicole Mobley. Pugh was charged with murdering the child Feb. 7. It talks about Pugh being out on a $25,000 bond. Ms. Mobley was not charged at this time. Other charges pending against Pugh include the burglary of a local residence Aug. 4. Bond was set for the burglary charge for $5,000.

Bond Set In Burglary Cases

Warner Robins — *Bond for a Warner Robins man and a Macon man charged Thursday with burglary has been set at $5,000 each.*

Warner Robins police arrested John Ricky Pugh, 28, of 307 Arrowhead Trail, Warner Robins, and William Edward Shupe, 28, of Ridge Road, Macon, Tuesday morning, shortly after they allegedly attempted to burglarize a house at 101 Gordon St.

Pugh, who was freed two months ago on a $25,000 bond for a voluntary manslaughter charge, also faces a violation of probation charge, stemming from a DeKalb County incident. He is being held without bond in Houston County Jail. Shupe also remains in the Houston County Jail at this time.

Meanwhile, police continue searching for a woman believed to have been with the men when the burglary allegedly occurred about 8:30 a.m. Tuesday.

According to warrants taken out on Pugh and Shupe, the men broke a carport window at the Gordon Street house, and Shupe entered the residence, setting off a burglar alarm. The suspects fled the scene in a car, and were picked up by police a short time later after a witness gave officers the tag number and description of the getaway vehicle, WRPD Detective Galen Noll said.

Pugh and Shupe were arrested at 129 Robinhood Drive, according to Noll. Nothing was taken in the burglary.

The case remains under investigation by Noll and WRPD Detective Charles Sadio.

Pugh was originally charged with murder in connection with the Feb. 8 death of 2-year-old Dana Nichole Mobley. Ms. Mobley and Pugh shared a North Fifth Street residence at the time of the incident.

The murder charge was reduced to voluntary manslaughter and bond was set at $25,000 during a Feb. 20 commitment hearing. The pending case has not been presented to a Houston County grand jury, but Houston County District Attorney Theron Finlayson said Thursday he plans to bring the charge before a grand jury within the next 60 days.

The child's body was discovered by her mother in their apartment about 1 a.m. Feb. 8. Miss Mobley was transported to the Warner Robins-Houston County Hospital where she was pronounced dead. An autopsy was performed later that day, and the cause of death was determined to be severe internal injuries.

Man, Free on Bond, Arrested in Connection With Burglary:

Warner Robins — *A Warner Robins man, free on a $25,000 bond for a voluntary manslaughter* *charge, was arrested along with another man in connection with a Tuesday morning burglary.*

John Ricky Pugh, 28, of 307 Arrowhead Trail, who was originally charged with murder in connection with the Feb. 8 death of his girlfriend's 2-year-old daughter, was picked up by police Tuesday along with William E. Shupe, 27, of Route 1, Ridge Road, Macon. Both men will be charged with burglary today, according to Detective Galen Noll of Warner Robins Police Department.

Police also are looking for a woman, who may have assisted in the attempted burglary of a residence at 101 Gordon St. Tuesday.

According to a WRPD report, officers received a call about 8:30 a.m. that a burglary was in progress on Gordon St. Officers at the scene said a window at the residence was broken and the house burglar alarm had been activated.

A neighbor gave investigators the tag number and description of a vehicle that had just left the residence, the report said. Patrol units spotted the vehicle on Kimberly Drive and followed it to 129 Robinhood Drive where officers arrested Pugh and Shupe.

Nothing was taken from the Gordon Street residence, according to Noll.

"The burglar alarm went off about 10 seconds after the window was broken, and the burglars took off." He said. "They didn't have time to take anything.

The two suspects were transported to the Houston County Sheriff's Department this morning. Bond for Shupe has not been set, and Pugh, who faces a violation of probation warrant, will be held without bond. (Never)

The case remains under investigation by Noll and Detective Charles Sadio of WRPD.

Pugh was released from jail about two months ago on a $25,000 bond set by Justice of the Peace Nick Lazaros during a commitment hearing Feb. 20. Also, during that hearing, the murder charge against Pugh was reduced to voluntary manslaughter.

The pending case has not yet been presented to a Houston County District Attorney Theron Finlayson said this morning that he plans to bring the charge before a grand jury within the next 60 days.

Pugh was arrested Feb. 8 in connection with the death of Dana Nicole Mobley of 404-1 North Fifth Street.

Both {ugh and the child's mother, Debra W. Mobley, resided at the North Fifth St. residence at that time.

The child's body was discovered by her mother in their apartment about 1 a.m. Feb. 8. Miss Mobley was transported to the Warner Robins-Houston County Hospital where she was pronounced dead. An autopsy was performed later that day, and the cause of death was determined to be severe internal injuries.

During Pugh's commitment hearing, Warner Robins Police Detective Timothy McGee, who investigated the child's death, testified that there were "about 15 to 20 bruise marks on the child's body" the night of her death.

The District Attorney stated they would bring charges before a Grand Jury within 60 days. Well, guess again Dixie! Not only did the charge not go before the Grand Jury within the 60 days, they did let Pugh out on bond. He is free to go on and commit other crimes.

Another article: Finally, in September, which was much, much later than 60 days, Pugh went before the Grand Jury. (I cannot help but wonder who is behind all this.)

Grand Jury Hands Down Murder Indictments for 3:

The article read. *Pugh and Debbie were indicted for the murder of Nikki. Pugh was charged with murder, but the charge was later reduced to voluntary manslaughter during a hearing before Justice of the Peace Nick Lazaros. Another reason for me to think something was going on that I did not know about. Debbie was not charged at this time. The article stated that other charges that were pending against Pugh included the burglary of a local residence Aug. 4th. Bond was set for the burglary charge at $5,000 following a probation revocation hearing in which Houston County State Court Judge, Paul Armitage ruled against revoking his 12-month probation sentence stemming from a bad check charge last January. He was later released on the additional $5,000 bond.*

AGAIN.

Couple faces new charges in death of 2-year-old girl:
New charges have been filed against a Warner Robins man and woman who were indicted for murder in September by the Houston County Grand Jury in connection with the death of a 2-year-old girl.

John Ricky Pugh, 29, and Debra Mobley, 22, also were indicted for cruelty to children in connection with the Feb. 7 death of Ms. Mobley's daughter, Dana Nicole Mobley.

The cruelty charge was added to the indictment so that, if convicted, the defendants could face more severe sentencing, said District Attorney Theron Finlayson.

Finlayson said he expects the case to be tried in January.

Chapter Ten

On my visits home from the hospital with Randy, I would read the articles that had been mailed to me from Warner Robins. There must be over a hundred articles that were in the papers from all over.

Accused Child Killer is Arrested
— *A Warner Robins man who failed last week to appear in Houston County Superior Court on February 1981 charges of murder and cruelty to children was arrested Thursday on a charge of violation of probation.*

John Ricky Pugh, 29, of 307 Arrowhead Trail, is being held without bond in the Houston County Jail, awaiting his trial which was rescheduled for Feb. 22, according to Houston County Sheriff's Department Officials. (To my knowledge, Pugh was never held in jail).

Pugh, who recently was picked up on undisclosed charges in Mobile, Alabama, was returned here last week by local officials. He was arrested in Warner Robins Feb. 8, 1981 on a murder charge, later reduced to voluntary manslaughter, in connection with the death of his girlfriend's 2-year-old daughter, Dana Nichole Mobley.

The child's body was discovered by her mother, Debra W. Mobley, in their Fifty Street apartment about 1 A.M. Feb. 8. According to an autopsy report, the little girl died of severe internal injuries.

Pugh was released from jail on a $25,000 bond in June 1981, and two months later he was arrested with another man on burglary charges here. Court Judge Paul Armitage ruled against revoking Pugh's 12-month probation sentence, stemming from a bad check charge in January 1981. Pugh later was released on the additional $5,000 bond.

Last September a Houston County grand jury indicted both Pugh and Ms. Mobley on murder charges in connection with the child's death. According to that joint indictment, the couple inflicted multiple blunt traumatic injuries on the little girl, resulting in her death.

The two were re-indicted in December on the murder charge, and a charge of cruelty to children was added to the indictment.

Pugh also faces 14 charges of writing bad checks, and his bond for those counts total $2,100. He is scheduled to appear in Houston County State Court March 4-5.

Again, so much they say contradicts them. One time they are saying "held without bond," next time he is "out on bond." The last straw for me is when the authorities arrested him in Alabama for trying to steal a car. The paper states his arrest in Alabama was for failing to appear in court. One article stated the police apprehended him in Alabama for undisclosed charges. I always thought if awaiting trial on murder charges, you could not leave the state. I suppose rules only apply when it is convenient.

After hearing of his capture in Mobile trying to steal a car, I called authorities in Warner Robins and threw a fit. I told them if they were trying to let him escape without a trial for Nikki's murder, why did they not just buy him a plane ticket and send him wherever he wanted to go and stop the torture of our family waiting for a trial. It will soon be a year since Nikki's murder and no progress is been made. I know I was extremely busy taking care of Randy, but now we have to get all this pain and suffering behind us, and the only way we can is if we get the trial over.

I made several more phone calls, and could tell that no one was in any hurry to do anything. (Back then, people went on trial much sooner than they do now.) I placed a call to the District Attorney and he did a conference call with a Judge with our conversation and I told them if they did not try this case very soon that I would be in Warner Robins with a hundred of my family and friends and we would march down the main street with posters that would state that "this town will not bring to trial someone arrested for murder a year ago, and let him continue to commit other crimes". They were just letting him run loose to commit other crimes as he saw fit, for which to my knowledge, they never tried him. Very soon after that call, I received a call saying the trial had been set for February 22, 1982.

Chapter Eleven

Going back to the area where she was murdered was torture enough. I had not been back but one time since I left Donny's when I took him back after the funeral, and that was when Debbie's mother died 12 days after Nikki's death.

I have many friends still there, but I cannot bear to visit them.

Henry and I made our hotel reservations for the night before the trial. We wanted to be sure nothing would get in the way of being there the first thing in the morning. I had a very bad night before the trial. Henry said I cried and yelled all night long in our room.

Sitting through the trial was almost as hard as going through Nikki's funeral. The first day was choosing the Jury. I had never been in court before with a Jury, and all this was very painful for me. The second day was almost as painful as going through the funeral, maybe more so as we learned so much more than we knew the year before. The doctors called to testify received pictures to view regarding the case, as it had been so long since the incident. They would turn the pictures over to read information on the back, therefore exposing the actual picture right in front of us showing her badly bruised little body.

I felt so helpless, and was feeling pain for Donny and Debbie. I looked back and saw Debbie peeping through a small glass in the door. Since called to testify, she could not be in the courtroom during the trial. My heart went out to her. She would not testify today.

She had gone through all this, and to have her charged in the beginning. I think part of the reason people were so down on her was because in the beginning she said she did not believe Pugh killed Nikki, yet we had this baby that was dead, so "someone had to have killed her", and Pugh kept stating that he did not know what could have happened. You are not left in charge of a 2-year-old child, have the baby beaten to death, and not know what happened. Yet he maintained no one else came by the apartment except the ones he mentioned.

Chapter Twelve

I had the transcript of the trial for about ten years before I was able to read it. In part, it mentions the cause of death was a couple of tears in the mesentery caused by someone stomping her. It mentions that death occurred within three to six hours after the infliction of the injury in their opinion.

In the investigation, it reads that Mr. Pugh stayed with the child alone after Debbie's sister left. Another man had come by and apparently exchanged a marijuana cigarette. It was interesting that Ricky Pugh never mentioned that to the police that night.

Officer Mofford, one of the officers there that night testified that he was at the 7-11 store approximately one-thirty when Debbie came in, obviously upset and said her child could not breathe and she needed help. He responded. Mrs. Purvis who was there also responded and attempted to resuscitate the child. The child was dead by then.

Then comes the two crucial witnesses for the state: Drs. Whitaker and Dr. Howard, two gentlemen that are experts in their field, don't know Ricky Pugh from Adam, have no, absolutely no interest in this case, and they're only going to testify as to what cold, logical science indicates, and what did they testify to?

Dr. Whitaker, who has performed over a thousand different autopsies, testified in over four courts, four states in court, testified that at the autopsy he discovered a tear in the mesentery of this child.

When that was torn, the child essentially bled to death internally over time. Death was not immediate. The reason that they know that death was not immediate is because of the hemorrhage, the fact that clotting had taken place. Clotting does not take place after death.

Both doctors agreed that the injury would have had to occur by the child placed against a hard surface and tremendous pressure applied to the abdomen from front to back.

Dr. Whittaker stated that the only way, in his opinion, accidentally it could have occurred is being strapped in an automobile going 60 miles an hour and having rapid deceleration like hitting a brick wall. Tremendous force caused the injury.

Also during the trial, another family came by to get some things left in the apartment. The room Nikki was in had the door closed and the light off. The mother came back in and told Pugh that something was wrong with the child, and she had vomited on herself. Pugh goes and wipes the child off, pulls the door back to and cuts the light out, and says, to the effect, it is that damn Tylenol.

It is amazing the contradictions and omissions that Mr. Pugh failed to tell the officers about at that time.

The following afternoon, at 1:45 Pugh was advised that he was a suspect in a murder, and I think at that point in time any reasonable person, if you're going to talk to the police, you're going to tell pretty much everything you know, and if there's a suspect, if you didn't do it and if there's another person that could have done it, you're going to let them know that. He did not mention the family coming by, he never mentioned leaving the child alone, or going on an errand, said the officers. Moreover, certainly did not mention Davey Whitten coming by.

A man, we're talking about an injury inflicted, according to Dr. Whitaker, consistent with stomping, a man that has had some karate training by his own admission involving kicking with feet, a man that enjoys wrestling, that watched wrestling, a man that consumes drugs, marijuana, he smoked it that day. Only one person, ladies and gentlemen, could have and did inflict those wounds; that is Ricky Pugh. Why? I do not know. I cannot tell you why in the world anyone would want to hurt a two-and-a-half-year-old child, but look at these photographs.

Mr. Pugh's conduct was interesting when he got back that night from picking Debbie from work. He dressed the child for bed; put the child in bed himself. Obviously, I do not think he wanted the mother to touch the child, to see the child, probably hoping that the child would recover, said the attorney.

Why had Pugh not gotten help? He said he bathed her around nine o'clock. He had to know, he did not act, and I think that is damming in and of itself, said the prosecuting attorney.

Then they called Debbie's sister to the stand. She was the last one to see Nikki alive late that afternoon.

Next, the police officer that was at the Seven-eleven store when Debbie ran into there testified. There was also another woman in there that night. She said that Debbie was too upset to drive, so they drove her home and performed CPR on Nikki, but it was too late.

74

Several other doctors testified, and questioned if, in their opinion, if a two-and-a-half-year old child playing or stumbling and falling on something could have caused that type of injury. He was testifying to the tears in the mesentery. They said it could not.

"Ladies and gentlemen, we are going to take this opportunity to recess for the day. During the overnight recess, of course, you should not discuss the case among your family or friends or with others. You should not make any effort to learn anything about the case outside the courtroom. You should read no newspaper article concerning the case nor permit anyone to discuss such with you. You should not listen to any radio account or watch any television account of the trial or of the facts of the case," instructed the Judge.

The next day the manager of the Pizza Hut where Debbie worked testified. She verified that Debbie was in fact at work from 4 PM until 10 PM that night.

Next, the family that went to the apartment that afternoon testified. It was a mother, father, and two children. One of the children testified that when he went into the room, Nikki was lying with her head between two pillows. And she had vomited; it was puddle on both sides of her neck. She was lying there with her eyes were wide open. "My mother asked Ricky to come in and clean her up. He came in there, got a towel, and wiped her face off." He looked at a picture of Nikki to be sure it was she in the bed.

The prosecutor asked, "Was the child was covered up.?" "Yes, sir, she was covered up to her neck," replied the witness. "What was Ricky was doing when they arrived at his apartment?"

"He was watching wrestling."

Next Debbie was on the stand, the question was asked: the day after this incident happened, when you and Ricky were on route to the hospital, at the autopsy did Mr. Pugh say anything to you along the lines of "this would just make us closer or get us closer together?" Yes.

Ricky Pugh was called to the stand. He was questioned again if anyone else other than the ones mentioned had been at the apartment that afternoon. He said they had not been anyone else there. Still not mentioning Davey was there.

In the end of the trial: As you have been previously told, members of the jury, the defendant, John Ricky Pugh, was indicted on December 7, 1981, by the grand jury of this circuit; and in that indictment he was charged in two counts. In the first count, he was charged with the murder of Dana Nicole Mobley, and in count two of that indictment, he was charged with committing the offense of cruelty to children on the same minor child.

After you consider all the facts and circumstances in the case, if your minds are wavering, unsettled and unsatisfied then that is the doubt of the law, and you should acquit the defendant. On the other hand, if such doubt does not exist in your mind as to his guilt, you should convict him.

You may retire.

THE COURT: Mr. Finlayson does the state have any exceptions to the charge? "No, sir, your Honor."

THE COURT: "Does the defendant at this time, Mr. Lee, Your Honor, just one. The charge as given relating to the lesser included offense of felony murder, we except to that because it might tend to indicate to the jury that there would be a lesser penalty for that offense and might affect their deliberations one way or another."

"Other than that, I don't have any other exceptions at this point. However, I do have a motion I want to make for the record; and I move for a mistrial on the grounds that during the closing argument, The District attorney referred to the fact that Donny Mobley was sitting in the front row of the spectators over there, and that he had had to bury his child. That was not a matter which was brought up in this case. I feel like it was intended to put pressure on the jury to arrive at a certain verdict, and I feel that the court should declare a mistrial in the matter."

THE COURT: "Motion denied."

RECHARGE OF THE COURT: "In response to your request, members of the jury, I'm simply going at this time to re-instruct you concerning the offenses of malice murder and felony murder."

"Before I do that, I want to point out that it was brought to my attention earlier that when I first mentioned the offense of felony murder as being an offense that you could consider under the first count of the indictment, I referred to it as a lesser included offense of malice murder, and that was an error on my part. Felony murder is simply another type of murder which you are authorized, along with malice murder, to consider under the charge of count one of the indictment."

"First, I will redefine for you the offense of malice murder. A person commits murder when he unlawfully with malice aforethought, either express or implied, causes the death of another human being. Express malice is that deliberate intention unlawfully to take away the life of a fellow creature, which is manifested, or shown, by external circumstances capable of proof. Malice shall be implied where no considerable provocation appears and where all the circumstances of the killing show an abandoned and malignant heart. A wanton and reckless state of mind may be the equivalent of a specific intent to kill. Malice is an essential ingredient of murder, and it must exist before any homicide can be malice murder."

"Malice in its legal sense is not necessarily ill will or hatred. It is the unlawful, deliberate, preconceived intention to kill a human being without justification or mitigation or excuse, which intention must exist at the time of the killing. It is not necessary, however, that this unlawful, deliberate intention exists for any particular length of time before the killing. If it enters the mind of the slayer a moment before he commits the fatal act that is sufficient."

"Felony murder is defined as follows: A person commits the crime of murder when, in the commission of a felony, he causes the death of another human being irrespective of malice. Cruelty to children is a felony, and if you find beyond a reasonable doubt that the defendant committed that felony, namely, cruelty to children, you would be authorized to consider the matter of felony murder."

"Since I have already defined for you the offense of cruelty to children, I will not redefine that at this time."

"In order for a homicide to have been done in the perpetration of a felony, there must be a direct connection between the felony and the homicide. It would not be enough to find the defendant guilty of the commission of a felony. You must also find beyond a reasonable doubt that the death resulted directly from the commission of the felony. It is not enough that the homicide occurred soon or presently after the felony. You must find that the act of the defendant to committing the felony, if he did so, was the proximate cause of the death of the victim."

"In order for the felonious act of a defendant to be the proximate cause of the victim's death, it must be shown that the act itself constituted the sole proximate cause of the death or that the act directly and materially contributed to the happening of a later immediate cause of death."

"In felony murder it is not essential that the defendant intended to kill the victim, but it is essential that he intended to commit the felonious act which cause or contributed to the death."

"Therefore, if you find beyond a reasonable doubt that the victim's death was a direct result of injuries caused by the felonious set of the defendant, then you would be authorized to convict the defendant of felony murder; and that would be true even if you found the defendant did not intend to kill the victim."

"Of course, in a malice murder you must find a specific intent to kill."

"Members of the jury that will conclude these additional instructions to you. I caution you to remember that I have previously instructed you on other areas of the law which pertain to this case; and it would be your duty in deliberating the case to apply all of the law I have given you in my instructions to you, remembering that I am giving you these additional instructions simply at your request."

"You may retire to the jury room." The jury retired at 3:35 p.m. The jury returned at 3:49 p.m.

"Your Honor, the verdict as to count one: We find the defendant guilty of felony murder. As to count two: We find the defendant guilty of cruelty to children."

"The sentence in a murder case, of course, is mandated by statue; and where the state does not seek the death penalty, the only penalty that can be imposed by the court is life imprisonment. "

"As I have already said, there is only one sentence the court can impose; and that is to say, I now sentence you, Mr. Pugh, to confinement under the supervision of the board of corrections of this state for and during the balance of your natural life. "

Well, we shall see…

Chapter Thirteen

The articles in the paper begin.

Pugh Trial Begins:
Perry — Two pathologists testifying Monday in the trial of a Warner Robins man accused of murder and cruelty to children said that the 2-year-old victim was probably stomped to death.

Dr. James Whitaker, Houston County medical examiner, said the autopsy performed on Dana Nicole Mobley Feb. 8, 1981, reveled that the child bled to death from blows to the abdomen that caused two tears in the mesentery membrane.

He said force exerted from the blows from the front of her midsection to the back caused two bruises on her face from her vertebrae, indicating that the child's back was against a hard surface when she was struck.

John Ricky Pugh, 29, of 307 Arrowhead Trail, is charged along with the girl's mother, Debra W.

Mobley, with the death of the child and cruelty to children.

Ms. Mobley, who had custody of the small child from an earlier marriage, was living with Pugh in a Fifth Street apartment at the time of the incident.

Sheri Whitten, Ms. Mobley's sister, testified that the last time she saw the child was at 4:15 P.M. February 7, 1981, and the child was fine except for suffering from a slight cold.

She said Pugh, who did not have a job, took care of the child often, and was doing so that day.

She said she had never seen Ms. Mobley or Pugh abuse the child.

"Ricky spent a lot of time with her — they got along good', said Ms. Whitten.

Warner Robins Police Officer Anthony Moffitt testified that at 1 A.M. Feb. 8, 1981, Ms. Mobley ran in to a convenience store on Watson Boulevard asking for help because her baby had stopped breathing.

A customer in the store, Ms. Daphene Purvis, testified that she went to the home with Ms. Mobley while the officer called an ambulance.

Having just completed a cardiopulmonary resuscitation course, Ms. Purvis said she began to perform CPR on the baby but received no response from the baby.

During the autopsy, Whitaker said he also examined several bruises on the baby's body.

"A great deal of force" caused the two tears that caused the baby to bleed to death, he said.

He said the child was probably lying on her back on the floor and an individual jumped or stepped on her.

Under cross-examination by defense attorney Joneal Lee, Whitaker said it could not have been accidental because of the amount of force used. He said it was as if the child was sitting in a car with a seat belt on and the car crashed going approximately. 60 mph. That kind of force could cause a tear in the mesentery membrane and cause internal bleeding, he said.

Dr. Larry Howard, director of the state crime lab in Atlanta, corroborated this testimony of Whitaker about the time of the incident.

By examining tissue slides, Howard estimated the fatal injuries took place three to six hours before the death of the child at 1 A.M. on Feb. 8.

Howard said the cause of death could not have been accidental because the "trauma was repeated." The two bruises on the back and the two tears in the mesentery indicated there were two blows struck.

In opening statements, Houston County District Attorney, Theron Finlayson said the state would prove that the death of Miss Mobley "was not accidental but deliberate. John Ricky Pugh inflicted the wounds on the child, causing her death."

Pugh Gets A Life Sentence:

Perry — A 29 year-old Warner Robins man was given the mandatory sentence of life in prison Tuesday for felony murder and cruelty to children for the death of 2-year-old Dana Nicole Mobley Feb. 8, 1981.

Houston County Superior Court Judge Willis B. Hunt, Jr. handed down the sentence to John Ricky Pugh following the guilty verdict rendered by the jury of seven men and five women after two hours of deliberations.

Pugh and co-defendant Debra W. Mobley, the child's mother, was indicted last year on a two-county indictment for murder and cruelty to children.

The charges against Ms. Mobley, the mother of the child, are still pending.

Houston County District Attorney, Theron Finlayson said his office will review the evidence produced at this trial and make a determination for the disposition of the case against Ms. Mobley.

Referring to the verdict in the Pugh case, Finlayson said he was pleased. "Hopefully this will place other individuals on notice that prosecutors and juries will look harshly on cases involving children as victims of crime."

A devout wrestling fan, the defendant said he was watching wrestling on television that afternoon and had smoked half of a marijuana cigarette. He said he had also had a few karate lessons.

During the cross-examination, Finlayson asked Pugh if the child, who was suffering from a slight cold, had possibly bothered him or began to cry while he was watching television.

Pugh responded, "No".

This led to the prosecution's contention that Pugh was probably watching the program and in an effort to quite her struck her several times.

Asked by defense attorney Joneal Lee to tell of her finding the child dead, Ms. Mobley paused and began to cry.

She said she went into the bedroom at about 1 A.M. to lay down with the child.

Ms. Mobley said she tried to get the child up to make room for herself on the bed.

"She didn't move. She was stiff," she said.

Ms. Mobley told the jurors she called Pugh, who picked up the baby and said "she's dead."

She said she then left to call for help.

Earlier Ms. Mobley said when she returned from work at 10 P.M. the baby appeared "sleepy and weak."

She said the baby would not eat and while getting the baby ready for bed, she noticed bruises on the baby and questioned Pugh about them.

Pugh told her, she testified, that the baby fell against a footstool earlier that day. The defendant also stated that in his testimony.

County Releases Mother In Daughter's Murder

Houston County officials, who already have obtained a conviction of a man on murder and cruelty charges for the death of a 2-year-old girl, will not prosecute the child's mother. After a review of the evidence and testimony produced at the trial of Pugh, who was convicted of both murder and cruelty to children, I feel the state could not successfully prosecute Debra Mobley on similar charges.

Robins man sentenced to life for child's death

Perry — Arms folded across his chest, a Warner Robins man listened calmly Tuesday as he was sentenced to life in prison for the murder of his girlfriend's 2-year-old daughter.

The conviction of John Ricky Pugh, 29, came after 90 minutes of deliberation by a Houston County Superior Court jury on murder and cruelty charges. The verdict followed nearly a full day of emotional testimony surrounding the Feb. 7, 1981 slaying of Dana Nicole Mobley.

Among those testifying the second day of the trial was the girl's mother. Debra Whitten Mobley, who tearfully recounted finding the child's bruised body. Mrs. Mobley, 22, also is charged with murder and cruelty stemming from the death of the infant, who physicians testified earlier was beaten to death.

86

Donny Mobley, Ms. Mobley's ex-husband and the child's father, had tried to obtain custody of the child on several occasions, according to the child's grandmother, Dixie Mobley Short. She, along with other family members, including the child's father, watched all court proceedings.

The child died of internal bleeding caused by two strong blows, according to medical examiners. The blows were inflicted during evening hours when Pugh was alone watching the child while Mrs. Mobley was at work according to testimony.

Taking the stand as a defense witness Tuesday, Mrs. Mobley testified Pugh picked her up from work and she found the baby in the back seat of the car. She said the child appeared listless and did not acknowledge her presence. She said she thought the child was "getting sicker" because she had a cold and had just had a tonsillectomy.

Mrs. Mobley said when she returned home from work and dressed the child for bed, she found bruises on her back and stomach.

"Risky said she had fallen on the ottoman", she said.

Pugh testified, "She fell against an ottoman after her bath. Her feet were wet and she stumbled backwards. She more or less slipped."

Physicians testified Monday the injuries could not have been caused accidentally because of the force required to tear the internal organs.

In testimony Monday, Dr. James Q. Whitaker, a Houston County medical examiner, said the injuries were probably caused when someone stood on the child's abdomen while she was lying on a hard surface such as a floor.

Houston County District Attorney Theron Finlayson suggested in closing arguments that Pugh, a professional wrestling fan who had knowledge of karate, may have become emotionally involved in a match on television and struck the child. Pugh admitted to Finlayson he had been smoking marijuana that evening.

Mrs. Mobley testified that although she had never seen Pugh abuse her child, Pugh had on occasion struck her in anger.

"Maybe I struck her in self-defense in a lover's quarrel," Pugh said.

Pugh was sent to a prison in a South Georgia town in Wayne County. It is almost unbelievable what happened down there.

Chapter Fourteen

Now, finally does this mean that our lives can begin once more to try to heal, and I can get back to see about Randy and get him well and all of us get on with our lives?

"Well think again, Dixie…"

Donny moved up to Snellville to try to get his life together again. We all felt he could get over the trauma if he were to get away from where it all happened, avoid the constant reminders, and not know Pugh was walking the streets free as a bird.

But after several months, preferring to return to work, he decided to move back to Warner Robins. Maybe, just maybe, things can start looking better for all of us.

It was getting near to Christmas. Maybe this Christmas can be a little better than last Christmas. It will be the second Christmas without Nikki. I was sad, hurt, and angry that we did not have her with us. It was just not fair. She should be here opening presents with us, instead of me decorating a small tree with little presents all over it and taking it to place on her grave.

I had placed a candle in the window on Christmas Eve the year before, and this year the President had asked everyone to place a candle in the window in honor of all the military men. I was upset, not that I did not want to remember the military men; I was afraid she would not be able to find hers.

I had started placing a rose on her grave on the 7th of the month from the beginning. As I left work on December 6, I was going to a mall to do some Christmas shopping. Christmas is still very hard for me, although all holidays are sad for me. I stopped at a florist to purchase a "pink" rose to place on her grave the next day. As I started up the freeway to the mall, I felt as though a magnet was pulling me back home.

The further I drove, the more I felt pulled to go back home. By now, after so much has happened in my life, and I have had these feelings so often recently, I decided I should turn around and go home. When I got there, no one was home.

It had been several months now without a major incident, yet I felt as though my world was just beginning to start spinning too fast for me once again. I turned on the TV and just decided to wait and see what it was that I was sent back home for. What now? What else could happen to me?

On the TV, they were showing a baby that was having a problem. I had adjusted myself to avoid looking at babies, especially the ones at her age, as it was just too painful. I remember that just seeing a glimpse of the baby made me start to cry.

In just a very short while, the phone rang. Here it comes! I felt so strongly that this call would tell me why I was pulled back home. It was Debbie. She told me that Pugh had called her and he had been "accidentally released from Prison." "What do you mean he has been accidentally released? He was placed there for life, and I thought that he would have to spend at least seven years at best, before being considered for release." He had only been there from the end of February to first of December. Enough time has not passed for us to be prepared for him to be free. Debbie seemed very upset over this also.

Again, my first thoughts were of Donny. I have to call and tell him before he hears it from someone else. When I called Donny, he told me he was just thinking about calling me, as so often when one called the other that was what we each had just been thinking. When I told him about the accidental release of Pugh, he told me he had awakened in the middle of the night just recently and thought to himself what he would do if Pugh ever got out of jail. I do not think he could have lived in the same town as Pugh should he decide to come back to his Father's house in Warner Robins, and I would not have felt comfortable for him to be in the same town with Donny.

The more I thought of what Debbie told me, the more upset I became. This was just not fair. I called the Wayne State Prison. They told me "the paper work just slipped through a crack," and that written on the front of his folder he was in prison for life for murder, but someone there thought he was just in for stealing. I asked them if they had issued a warrant to go get him. They had not. They did not appear as though they were going to do anything immediately. In fact, they told me he would eventually commit another crime and they would catch him.

Debbie also told me that when Pugh called her he said he was at his mother's in Mobile, Alabama. I did not think that he would stay at his father's in Warner Robins as too many people had expressed after the trial it would not be good for him to return to that area.

I remembered that there was a phone number on one of the local TV Stations that would get you in touch with an investigative reporter that could help you if someone treated you unfairly, or if you had any problems of interest. I called the number, and someone at the station asked why I was so upset. I told him, and he said he would have someone call me. In just a matter of minutes, the call came and I asked them if they could help me get to the right person to get Pugh back in prison.

On the 11 P.M. news, they mentioned the accidental release of Pugh, and they had already contacted someone from the Pardon and Parole office. He made a statement on TV about the accidental release. This man from Pardon and Parole office showed very little concern and said, "The paper work just fell through a crack." I could tell from his statement that they were not going to do anything about getting him back. In fact, it seemed as though he had a smile on his face.

The next morning all over the news was the fact that two men had escaped from Reidsville Prison, and there was an "all out" hunt for them. I could not understand how they could be so concerned for those men that escaped, yet be so unconcerned for the one for which they held the door open.

I could not go into work the next day. I did not know what to do next. I started making my list of people I could call that might be able to give me some advice. Right now, all I could think of was the man that sent to prison for killing Nikki was set free after just nine months. It was too soon after the trial to accept this information.

During all this time, which lasted 34 days from the time of Pugh's release to the time of his capture, one of all the Atlanta TV stations was at my house almost every day carrying the story. The TV stations as well as the newspapers all over

Georgia are the ones that I give credit to for helping me through this terrible time, and letting DOR know that I was not going to fade away as they hoped I would.

I was just a little "nobody" from just a small little town.

Chapter Fifteen

Jim Axel from a local TV Station came out to my house the next day to see me and to do an interview. I had the pink rose I had purchased the night before on the kitchen counter. He asked me about it, and I told him I purchased one every month to place on her grave on the 7th which was that day. He asked if he could go to the cemetery with me, which he did.

All the media from all the TV stations were so nice and concerned.

Not knowing what to do next, I went back to work the next day as I thought perhaps just one person would cross my path that could help me, yet if I stayed at home, I would only have contact with the ones I was calling. If they did not get him soon, he may decide to hide somewhere else, and the authorities would not find him.

Luck was with me a few days later in December. An employee of the Gwinnett Daily News stopped by my office to pick up the advertisements. She asked me why I was so down. I explained to her my problem. She said she would ask at the paper if anyone knew who could help me get some answers.

A short while later, I received a call and was asked if someone there could come out and talk with me.

Of course, I would have talked with anyone. The Gwinnett Daily ran an article on the front page of the paper with my picture and a picture of Nikki and had a story of what had happened and why I was trying so desperately for help. For after that article, I began to get results as I was desperately trying to get someone to go for Pugh and put him back in prison, yet every law enforcement I spoke with told me they did not have the authority to send for him. It seemed to me that if the Department of Rehabilitation had the authority to issue the order for a release, and then realize they made a mistake, they could certainly issue the warrant to go and pick him up and return him to prison.

Once again, my suspicions were that some one was behind all this. It did not seem normal for them to let him go so many times prior to his trial. Yet, here the paper work just fell in a crack. I often wonder if this was someone's plan.

I believe the article in the local newspaper really helped get the ball rolling for me. It appeared on the front page and covered almost one fourth of the front page, and continued on to a page inside.

Dixie Short: Pictures and memories are all that remain of her only granddaughter.

"A Christmas Nightmare:
Dixie Mobley Short Won't Rest Until Killer is Jailed"

- Dixie Mobley Short's Christmas season is haunted by two unsettling images — the body of her murdered 2-year-old granddaughter and the accidental release from jail of the child's convicted murder.

On Feb. 23, John Ricky Pugh was convicted of the Feb. 7, 1981 stomping death of his girlfriend's child, Dana Nicole Mobley, and sentenced to life in prison. On Nov. 23, due to an apparent paperwork error, Pugh was released from the Wayne County prison facility in which he was housed.

The error was not realized until 13 days later when Pugh called the child's mother to tell her he was free.

Short, Nikki's paternal grandmother and a Snellville resident, had just returned home from purchasing a pink rose to place on the child's grave when she heard of Pugh's release.

"My first reaction was a total state of shock and disbelief that after I worried and struggled to get it brought to trial, he was released like that. It was more than I could handle", she said.

"Put yourself in the position of being a grandmother and having a beautiful 2 ½ year-old granddaughter actually stomped to death. And then they actually set him (Pugh) free. This I cannot accept."

State prison officials are calling the release a mix-up in paperwork. Incomplete records reportedly cited Pugh only with a parole violation and not with the murder.

To Nikki's grandmother, however, that answer is not definite enough.

"I want to know exactly where this mistake occurred. There has been a lot of professional buck-passing. Everyone is blaming everyone else. Then I want to know why it occurred. Then I want to know what the state is going to do about it. Those are the three main concerns other than getting Pugh back behind bars", Short said.

"If our system is so bad this paperwork can go down a crack, we need to know that," Short said. *A diminutive woman, Short sat in the conference room of the Gwinnett office where she is employed and displayed her key ring containing two pictures of Nikki. At 2, the child grinned from the photographs with a toothy smile.*

Short held the key ring tightly.

"I will get my answer," she said. *"I will find out why. If I have to, I'll go to Washington. If I have to, I'll stand on the street corner with a cup and beg for money to go to Washington. I couldn't do anything at all about him killing her, and I couldn't do anything about the trial because that's the law. But it doesn't look like the law is doing anything to put him back. I want him back in prison".*

On Dec. 6, Short called her former daughter-in-law, Debra W. Mobley, Nikki's mother to see how she was doing.

"My family would prefer if I just forgot Debbie existed," Short explained, *"but she is the mother of my only grandchild. I think if I hold onto Debbie, I can hold onto a little bit of Nikki."*

When Mobley answered the phone, she was in tears, Short said, *having called her attorney to inform him that Pugh was free.*

In a state of shock, Short called the Wayne County Prison and was told that the release was a mistake. "I kept thinking, "This mistake just cannot be."

Since Dec. 6, Short has been "going non-stop" trying to find the reason for the mistake. She has been in contact with the Governor's office, the Houston County District Attorney's office where Pugh was convicted and has been trying to contact the State Attorney General for help.

She said she has been receiving assistance from State Rep. elect Mike Barnett and State Sen. Ed Barker, whose district includes Warner Robins where the murder took place.

On Friday morning, Short said, a spokeswoman in the Houston District Attorney's office told Short they had received no offers from the state to help locate Pugh.

"I'm hearing nothing from the state," Short said.

Short's worries go past Pugh's accidental release, she said. She also saw in congruencies in the amount of time it took for Pugh to be put on trial for Nikki's death and the manner in which the state handled the time Pugh was out on bond.

Nikki was killed on Feb. 7, 1981, while Pugh was baby-sitting her in her Warner Robins home. Pugh was charged with the murder on Feb. 8, but the charge was later reduced to voluntary manslaughter and he was released on $25,000 bond. (No surprise to me).

In September 1981, both Pugh and the child's mother were indicted on murder charges. Two months later, they were re-indicted for cruelty to children. Mobley was never tried due to lack of evidence against her and because she provided evidence against Pugh.

By the time he was tried for the murder on Feb 22, 1982, Pugh had been arrested on burglary charges in Warner Robins, had been picked up on undisclosed charges in Mobile, Alabama, had been charged with a violation of probation, and faced 14 charges of writing bad checks.

"I want to know why," Short said. "I want to know why it took a year for him to be tried. We were watching him commit all those crimes in the meantime, but they kept letting him out. How can one person get away with so much and then accidentally be set free?"

"I want to be sure. It's inexcusable no matter where you look. I'm not accusing anyone, but I have doubts," she said.

Short said she would like a legislative investigation into the incident because of what it indicates about the condition of the state penal system.

"I will do this through Christmas. My Christmas is ruined. I know we are supposed to be celebrating the birth of Christ, but I'm suffering the death of Nikki. It's one beautiful baby for another, I suppose".

Short said there is no way to describe her love for her grandchild, who is buried up the road from her in Snellville. "Sometimes I wonder if I loved her too much," she said.

"I worshipped that child. I put a glass dome around her, and somebody broke it."

The heading read: **"A Christmas Nightmare: Dixie Mobley Short Won't Rest Until Killer is Jailed."** A picture appeared on the left of the article of Nikki. In the center was a picture of me that read underneath: It showed me sitting at my desk holding a picture of Nikki. The statement, *"On Dec. 6, Short called her former daughter-in-law, Debra W. Mobley, Nikki's mother to see how she was doing,"* was not accurate; Debbie called me.

After this article appeared in the paper, I felt a glitter of hope. At least now it seemed that someone might care. The next day I received a call at work from Jack Hamilton, Deputy Sheriff from Gwinnett County, who asked if he and Deputy Sheriff Willard Baxter could come to my home that evening to help me, and I should not be having to do all this myself.

They came as soon as I got home from work. I explained to them that I knew where Pugh was, but could not get anyone to accept the responsibility of getting him back in prison. They told me that if I did not get some help soon, that they would take vacation and go get Pugh on their own time. They also told me that they would bring me back a picture of where they buried him. These two men showed more compassion that anyone could imagine, and that was my ray of hope that let me go on.

I explained to them that I had an appointment on Monday with the State's Attorney General. I decided to wait until after Christmas before going to the State.

I was so upset, but decided not to ruin everyone else's Christmas although no one minded ruining mine.

Mr. Mike Barnette, State Representative, called me and said he heard I had an appointment with the Attorney General and asked if he could take me for my appointment. I had talked with Mr. Barnette on several occasions prior to this, and I was very happy for him to accompany me there.

In the meantime, one afternoon at work I had just gotten off the phone with someone, I do not remember whom, as I called so many people trying to get help, and I was very upset after the conversation because again it seemed no one from the State wanted to do anything to help me. Then I received a call from Jim Wooten from the Atlanta Journal.

I must have spilled over to him all my anger, because the article that came out in the paper the next day read:

The Atlanta Constitution

The Angry Grandmother From Snellville:
by Jim Wooten
It is a tiny little story in the newspaper, an inconsequential little story lost in the holiday shuffle, there briefly and then gone, poof, like the man the prison held for killing Dixie Short's granddaughter.

She understands holiday shuffles, does Dixie Mobley Short, and she will let this story fester until Christmas is past, but come Monday morning the grandmother from Snellville intends to raise torment. "I'll let everybody get through Christmas before I blow my stack."

But blow she will, vows Dixie Short, who has lined up a meeting with the state's Attorney General, and if necessary she will see the governor and if necessary her congressman and if necessary the president and if necessary the King of Siam and his cousin and uncle and maitre 'd, too.

She's had the bureaucratic apology. That won't do. She's had the official explanation about the papers shuffling back and forth. That won't do either. She wants the man who killed her two-year granddaughter back in jail where he belongs. That's all. But she would settle for less. She'd settle for knowing that somebody official wanted him back in jail, too, and was doing something, something concrete, to get him there.

They owe that to her. He was in jail, John Ricky Pugh, the man convicted in Houston County of beating her granddaughter to death. The state had him down at Wayne County Correctional institution in Odom, his file stamped that he was to serve a lift sentence for killing young Dana Nichole Mobley on Feb. 7, 1981.

Just before Thanksgiving of this year, however, Pugh was escorted out the door and sent on his way with the blessings of the State Department of Offender Rehabilitation. Had he kept running, nobody yet might know. Instead, he stopped to call the dead girl's mother, Mrs. Short's ex-daughter-in-law, his former girl friend, to tell her he was out. Everybody was stunned.

He had served barely nine months of the life sentence.

That was the catch. He had served none of the life sentence. The prison system thought he was in for criminal use of an article with an altered identification mark, a CB radio. His file was stamped that he was under life sentence, but the prison system thought that was in Clayton County. Clayton had sent him for the CB radio. Somebody at DOR called Clayton to ask about the life sentence. Nope, they said, no life sentence here. Go free, young man.

Houston County had forwarded Pugh's file to DOR following his conviction there — hence, the stamp — but DOR returned it to Houston when it received notice he would appeal, which he didn't.

All that doesn't matter to Dixie Mobley Short. It's a sloppy bureaucratic mistake and she understands it. What she wants them to do now is get Pugh back.

Houston has issued a bench warrant. That's not enough, she says. Unless he walks into a police station with proper identification and surrenders, a bench warrant won't get him back. She wants somebody looking for him, or at least sending out bulletins to other police agencies. Somebody, she wants somebody, to actually does something to capture John Ricky Pugh.

"I don't want their apologies," says Mrs. Short, "I want them looking for him."

It is not much for a grandmother to ask that the bureaucrats who turned her granddaughter's killer loose start the search to find him. But she will be patient until Christmas is past. Then the grandmother from Snellville goes to war. Woe, ye, bureaucrats.

The more articles I received and read from Macon and Warner Robins, only confirmed more strongly to me that my suspicions were accurate. Everyone it seemed wanted to blame someone else for the release instead of doing what was necessary to get him back in prison.

Chapter Sixteen

Father Relives Daughter's Tragedy

Warner Robins — For 25 year- old Donny Mobley, the accidental release of his daughter's convicted killer from the Georgia prison system is "like living the nightmare of her death all over again".

Mobley, who twice tried to gain custody of his 2-year-old daughter, Dana Nichole "Nikki" Mobley following his divorce from the child's mother in 1979, said he was "shocked and frustrated" to learn that the man responsible for his daughter's death was "walking the streets a free man."

John Ricky Pugh was convicted by a Houston County Superior Court jury last February for the 1981 beating death of young Nikki, who medical authorities said bled to death from blows to her abdomen. Pugh, who was living with the child's mother, Debra Mobley, was babysitting the toddler when she died.

Pugh was given a life sentence for the murder conviction, but due to a "paperwork mix-up" he was released from the Wayne County Correctional Institute on Nov. 23 by officials with the Department of Offender Rehabilitation.

"How many times must someone commit a crime before he must stay in jail?" Mobley asked after learning of Pugh's premature release. "There's something wrong with our legal system when a "paperwork mix-up" as this is called can allow a convicted murderer to go free after serving only a few months behind bars".

Mobley said his first reaction to the news was one of "anger and frustration. I just couldn't believe it," but now he says he feels confident that authorities will catch up with Pugh and return him to prison. "I know that there is justice somewhere, and he (Pugh) will be sent back where he belongs".

Mobley, whose home is Warner Robins, said he moved away for six months prior to and during Pugh's trial last February. "I tried to stay away because of the pressures I was feeling, but I ended up coming back for parts of the trial," he said. "Since then I've moved back to Warner Robins, and I've tried to rebuild my life, but this (learning of Pugh's release) just opens up terrible memories of Nikki's death and my attempts to win custody of my baby. It's just something I don't think I'll ever get over."

Authorities have placed a lookout for the 29-year-old Pugh, and Houston County District Attorney Theron Finlayson has obtained an arrest warrant for the convicted murderer.

According to a DOR spokeswoman, when Pugh's prison release was approved, prison officials were unaware that he had been sentenced to life for the murder. Pugh was freed after a five-year sentence he received in 1978 in Clayton County (for two counts of criminal use of an article with an altered identification number) was completed.

Officials learned of his mistaken release after Pugh called Debra Mobley and told her he was out of prison. Mobley said his mother, who was informed of the situation by Debra, told him about Pugh's release.

Memo from my files:

3:30 PM on December 20, 1082 I received this message:
Mr. Mickey Camp of DOR, Supervisor of Offender Administration, called me and informed me that Mr. Charlie Tidwell, Attorney for the Governor's Office whom I had been in contact with, asked him to call me and explain to me what

had happened in their office regarding the release of John Ricky Pugh.

Mr. Camp offered his apologies to me and said he would try to explain to me what took place.

After the trial, Houston County sent the papers of his life sentence to their office here at DOR, which they returned to Houston County when an appeal was filed.

He stated that although they sent the papers back to Houston County, there were keys in their files here, which they should have picked up on and they did not.

He said he was not trying to justify what has happened, that an error was made and unfortunately this is one that should never been made.

He apologized for himself and his staff. He stated it is a system failure, no more here than in Houston County, although he does not want to do any name calling.

I asked him what he was going to do about this error, was he going to insist the state put out more effort to correct this and apprehend Pugh and he said his office did not have that authority. I asked him to call me back and tell me who does and I would contact them next. He called me back and told me that would have to come from Houston County, and they did have a Nationwide Alert on the computer for Pugh on "Unlawful Flight."

This is not enough to satisfy me. I see and hear all they are doing to catch the ones that are escaping from Reidsville, but I do not see or hear about anything that is being done for the one they held the door open for.

I will not stop until I am satisfied — my son, Donny Mobley is there in Warner Robins whom I love very dearly and could not begin to know the pain and suffering he has gone through, as well as Nikki's mother and her family, and I will not stop until I feel I have reached the very end, and that is still very far away. I have to do this for my son.

10:30 AM, December 21, 1982, Senator Ed Barker, Warner Robins, called me and assured me that the DA, Judge, and Clerk of Superior Court in Houston County are doing everything they can to apprehend Pugh.

My appointment with the Attorney General; I will hope to see what action will be taken with the DOR, and hope and pray no one else will ever have to go through a horrible ordeal such as the murder, and never have to go through with an "accidental" release of the killer.

Houston Officials Deny Blame for Release of Killer:
A dispute among officials over responsibility for the accidental release of a convicted murderer continued Thursday as two Houston County officials said they are being wrongly blamed.

Houston County District Attorney Theron Finlayson and Clerk of Court Carolyn Sullivan summoned reporters and disputed comments by state prison officials that Houston County authorities were responsible for the release of John Ricky Pugh.

"They're trying to make it look like we didn't do our job." Declared Mrs. Sullivan, responding to a comment by a State Department Offender Rehabilitation spokeswoman that Houston County officials failed to submit paperwork that would have prevented Pugh's release.

Pugh was released from the State Prison System on November 23 after serving six months on a probation violation charge. State Prison officials said Pugh was released because they never were notified of his life sentence for the February 7, 1981 beating death of his girlfriend's 2-year-old daughter.

Pugh's release came to light after he called the slain child's mother, Debra Whitten Mobley, and said he had been released accidentally. Pugh remains at large, the subject of a bench warrant signed by Finlayson. The district attorney said Pugh is not considered dangerous. Excuse me; killing a baby is not dangerous).

On Thursday, Mrs. Sullivan provided reporters with documents she said show that Houston County Officials submitted written records of Pugh's life sentence to the DOR on March 26, which were stamped "received" by the DOR. The DOR returned the records a week later because Pugh's conviction was under appeal, she said.

Mrs. Sullivan also suggested that, after an error in DOR's records left prison officials unsure about where Pugh had been convicted, they should have made a greater effort to determine that it happened in Houston County.

"Why they didn't think to contact Houston County (before Pugh's release), I don't know. Houston County was where he had been when they picked him up from to go into the prison system anyway." Mrs. Sullivan said.

Finlayson said he was bothered because the state prison agency's spokeswoman, Paula Putney, says prison officials don't have the authority to apprehend Pugh because he was released legally.

"My main concern is getting him back in custody without anybody being hurt", said Finlayson.

Another article appeared:

It is no wonder I began to doubt the system. I felt from the beginning, even before the trial that someone was covering up something in Warner Robins.

It is no wonder that I was so upset and angry. Other articles started coming to me in the mail from Macon:

Prison Officials Blame Records Mix-up For Accidental Release of Child Killer:

Warner Robins — "A mix-up in paperwork was blamed Tuesday for the accidental release of convicted Houston County child murderer John Ricky Pugh, prison officials confirmed Tuesday.

The release of Pugh, who was serving a life sentence for the murder, only came to light after the convicted man's girlfriend said she received a call from Pugh over the weekend in which he told her he had been accidentally released.

Meantime, authorities issued a lookout for Pugh, and Houston County District Attorney Theron Finlayson, who prosecuted Pugh, issued a warrant for Pugh's arrest on escape charges.

Department of Offender Rehabilitation spokeswoman Meg Opdyche said Pugh was released from prison Nov. 23 because incomplete records showed only a parole violation and not the February conviction in the stomping death of his girlfriend's 2-year-old daughter.

"Apparently the DOR didn't notice their own notes and didn't even see the murder charge" when its board released Pugh from a Wayne County prison, said state Board of pardons and Paroles Deputy Director Silas Moore.

However, Ms. Opdycke disagreed, saying her agency was not formally notified by Houston County authorities of Pugh's conviction after he entered the prison system.

The victim's mother, Debra Mobley, who lives in Warner Robins, contacted an attorney Monday after receiving over the weekend a telephone call she said was from Pugh, who told her that he had been released by mistake.

Pugh, 29, was sentenced to life in prison by a Houston County jury in late February for the Feb. 7, 1981 stomping death of Dana Nichole Mobley.

DIXIE MOBLEY SHORT

Mrs. Mobley was indicted with Pugh on murder and child cruelty charges but not tried because of her testimony against Pugh and lack of evidence, according to Houston County District Attorney Theron Finlayson.

Jeff Grube, Mrs. Mobley's attorney during Pugh's trial, said his former client contacted him because she was "concerned and somewhat frightened" that Pugh had been released.

Grube said he believes Pugh may have made the call from Alabama, since "he has family there".

After the life sentence was imposed for the child's death, Pugh was taken to Clayton County in April for hearing on a probation revocation charge.

When he was sent into the state prison system in Wayne County on April 24, the accompanying paper work showed only the probation revocation sentence and not the murder charge, Moore said.

Houston County authorities sent copies of the sentencing order to the Board of Pardons and Paroles, but that paper work was returned to Houston County while a defense motion for a new trial was filed, according to Houston Assistant District Attorney James Garnett.

After the motion for a new trial was heard, the paper work containing Pugh's conviction for the slaying was returned to the Board of Pardons and Paroles, but apparently a mix-up allowed Pugh's release, Garnett said.

114

"Unfortunately, we were never notified the murder conviction stands, because our paper ssdc3qyhwork still shows his case as being under appeal', Ms. Opdycke said.

Pugh was assigned to prison in Wayne County only because that was where space was available, according to Garnett.

Garnett said he received a call from Grube on Monday asking if Pugh had been released. Garnett said he verified that indeed Pugh had been released and notified Warner Robins police and Houston County Sheriff's Department officials.

"All we can do is try them and place them in the (prison) system. What happens after that, we have no control of. It's really bizarre what happened," Garnett said.

Mrs. Mobley, 23, currently is living with her father.

During Pugh's trial, medical testimony showed that the child bled to death after she was struck twice in the abdomen with a "great deal of force".

Pathologists testified that the injuries occurred during nighttime hours, when Pugh, Mrs. Mobley's live-in companion, had exclusive custody of the child and Mrs. Mobley was at work.

Chapter Seventeen

Grandmother of Slain Child to See Busbee

December 11, 1982 Atlanta — The grandmother of a child whose convicted killer was accidentally released from prison last month said Friday she expects to meet with Gov. George Busbee to express her outrage.

Dixie Mobley Short, who lives in suburban Snellville, said a newly elected state legislator from Gwinnett County, Rep. Mike Barnett, has agreed to try to set up the meeting with Busbee.

At the meeting, which she understands may be the week of Christmas, Mrs. Short said she would ask the governor to order an investigation into the circumstances of the state Department of Offender Rehabilitation's release Nov. 23 of John Ricky Pugh.

Pugh was released from prison because officials said they were unaware of the life sentence he received for the beating death of Mrs.

Short's granddaughter, 2-year-old Dana Nichole Mobley.

Pugh, 29, who remains at large, was convicted last February in Houston County Superior Court for the Feb. 7, 1981 stomping death of the child. Houston County authorities learned of Pugh's release only after Pugh last week called the child's mother, Debra Whitten Mobley, who is Mrs. Short's ex-daughter-in-law.

Pugh had completed serving time on a probation violation in Clayton County when he was released from Wayne County Correction Institution.

"I don't understand how the Department of Offender Rehabilitation could let something like this happen", said Mrs. Short. "They should have had some kind of a backup system to double check so he couldn't be released".

Mrs. Short said she blames the DOR and not Houston County officials for what caused a paperwork mix-up that allowed Pugh's release.

"A man with the record he had, killing a child, should have drawn some attention to the case." She said. "I'm going to ask for a legislative investigation".

Mrs. Short, who viewed the child's beaten body in the Medical Center of Houston County's morgue and later arranged for Nichole's burial in a Gwinnett County cemetery, said she has been "tormented" by Pugh's release.

"After we went for a year knowing he killed our baby, then knowing he walked the streets until

the trial like he didn't owe anybody anything is more than I can take".

"I can't go through another time like that. I didn't ask for the death sentence and I don't know that I believe in capital punishment. But the fact that he's walking the streets now just isn't right".

The DOR said earlier this week that Houston County officials were to blame for not notifying prison officials of Pugh's murder conviction — a charge Houston County officials disputed with records Thursday.

Mrs. Short said her 26-year old son, Donny Mobley of Warner Robins, has been "devastated" that the convicted killer of his child has been released.

She said her son tried twice to gain custody of the child after his marriage with the Mobley woman broke up. Pugh was living with Mrs. Mobley when the slaying occurred.

Mrs. Short said she vividly remember the "stormy, stormy, Tuesday on Feb. 10, 1981 when Nichole was buried. "I still go out once a month and put a rose on her grave. She's still our little baby," she said.

Another article was in the Macon News stating that Dixie Mobley Short was to see the Attorney General after Christmas. News really traveled, and it was in many papers in the state.

December - State Representative Mike Barnette and I left out early the day after Christmas for my appointment to see the Attorney General.

When we arrived, he had a newspaper in his hand. He held it up and displayed the article that read: "The Angry Grandmother from Snellville." He also said, "I knew you were coming."

We talked for a great deal of time and I explained everything to him that I knew, what the officials from the prison had told me, what the Department of Rehabilitations had told me and explained that I was told that no one could issue the warrant to go out of state to bring Pugh back.

I also told him about my visit with Deputy Jack Hamilton and Deputy Willard Baxter; they had told me about taking vacation and getting him for me.

The Attorney General seemed very sympathetic to me. I cannot repeat what he told me he would do if he were I because Mr. Barnette is deceased and could not back up my statement, but I knew he genuinely cared.

The Attorney General issued the warrant that day to go for Pugh, and assigned the task to Mr. Hamilton and Mr. Baxter. I felt so relieved. I felt as though finally, now, someone cared about this terrible mistake.

He kept me posted on the process of going for Pugh. The first thing the detectives did was raid Pugh's father's house in Warner Robins. He was not there. Although, I already knew he was at his Mother's house in Mobile, Alabama. I was afraid after they went to his father's first, word would get to Alabama and he would leave.

As my luck would have it, that is exactly what happened. When they got to the home of Pugh's mother, he was not there. Another family member told the authorities that Pugh's mother had taken him to her parents in Louden, Tennessee when she got the word that they had raided Warner Robins. Mr. Hamilton and Mr. Baxter were afraid if they waited until they could go to Tennessee, word would beat them there, and Pugh would run again. Instead, they called the local postmaster there and got the address of Pugh's Grandparents. They then called the authorities in Tennessee and had them go out to arrest Pugh. They arrived in the middle of the night and arrested Pugh.

The authorities placed him in a prison in Lowden, Tennessee. There was no word of his extradition back to Georgia.

I felt his mother should have answered to someone for taking him out of state, as she had to have known he was not supposed to be free.

I received the following letter:

GEORGIA DEPARTMENT OF OFFENDER REHABILITATION

Dear Ms. Short:

Following your talk this week with Attorney General Michael Bowers, he inquired of this Department as to the status of the John Ricky Pugh case. In my reply to him, I advised that I would communicate personally with you on this matter.

During the month of March, 1982, a life sentence on Pugh was received at this department

120

from Houston County Superior Court. Since it was obvious that the case was in an appeal status and it was not within the authority of this Department to assume custody of such cases, the sentence was returned to the clerk of the court. Subsequently, during the month of April, Clayton Superior Court revoked the remainder of a probated sentence, which had been imposed for Criminal Use of an Article with Altered Identification Mark.

At the expiration of the Clayton County sentence, reviews occurred within this office seeking to ascertain the disposition of a life sentence reportedly from Clayton County. Obviously, Clayton County authorities were unable to furnish information as to that effect, and the individual was discharged from custody.

I am very personally distressed by the events which led to this incident, and I have cause the implementation of new procedures, which hopefully, will preclude a recurrence. A member of my staff has been designated to communicate with you immediately upon the re-apprehension of Pugh.

Signed: David C. Evans, Commissioner

The next day I received many phone calls after the news of Pugh's capture. They were from most of the people I had contacted.

Maybe my 34-day ordeal was worth all the begging and pleading to get Pugh back behind bars has worked. Most of them told me "the squeaking wheel gets the oil." I thought now this is over. Little did I know I would have one more battle to fight, returning him to Georgia.

Child-Killer Recaptured In Tennessee

Jan. 10, 1982 — Atlanta — *A convicted murderer who was inadvertently freed from the Georgia prison system in November was captured Sunday in Loudon, Tennessee, Georgia Bureau of Investigation Director Phil Peters said.*

Peters said John Ricky Pugh, 29, was taken into custody by Loudon County, Tenn., authorities after a GBI agent and a Gwinnett County deputy sheriff developed information indicating he was in the Loudon area.

Pugh, who was convicted of murdering a 2-year-old girl, was released from the Wayne County Correctional Institution Nov. 23 by state Department of Offender Rehabilitation Officials in what was described as "a paperwork mix-up."

He was convicted of murder Feb. 23 in Houston County in connection with the Feb.7, 1981, beating death of Dana Nicole Mobley. Houston County authorities were not aware that Pugh had been freed until he telephoned Debra Whitten Mobley, his former girlfriend and the mother of the victim, and told her he had been released.

Mrs. Mobley was unavailable for comment Sunday.

Peters said the GBI agent and the Gwinnett deputy went last week to Mobile, Alabama where Pugh's family lives. They were in Mobile early Sunday when they learned Pugh was in the Loudon area, he said.

The arrest was made by the Loudon County sheriff's office, Peters said. Authorities in Loudon refused Sunday to comment on how or where Pugh was captured. (He was captured at his grandmother's where his mother took him when she heard they were looking for him.)

Peters said Pugh has refused to return voluntarily to Georgia.

Houston County District Attorney Theron Finlayson said he would begin extradition proceedings this morning to bring Pugh back to serve the life sentence he received for the murder conviction.

Finlayson said the proceedings will involve proving that Pugh is wanted and proving that "he is, in fact, the person wanted."

Pugh was released on Nov. 23 after he completed serving a five-year sentence he had received in 1978 in Clayton County in connection with another case. Prison officials said that when his release was approved, they were unaware he had been sentenced to life for the murder of the Mobley child.

State prison system spokeswoman Meg Opdycke said Houston County officials notified the prison

123

system in April that Pugh had been convicted of murder and sentenced to life in prison.

But because Pugh was in the Houston County jail at the time, rather than in state custody, Ms. Opdycke said, the notice of his murder conviction and life sentence was returned to Houston County.

When Pugh subsequently was transferred to the state prison system to finish serving the sentence from Clayton County, state officials had no record of his murder conviction and life sentence, Ms. Opdycke said.

Another article the same day in the Atlanta paper on Jan. 10, 1982:

Grandmother Still Angry, But Relieved

Dixie Mobley Short remains "extremely upset" with state prison officials who refused to accept responsibility for the mistaken release of the man convicted of killing her granddaughter.

But Sunday afternoon, Mrs. Short was relieved to know John Ricky Pugh was again in custody and probably headed back to prison.

Pugh, 29, was arrested Sunday in Loudon, Tenn., after a Georgia Bureau of Investigation agent and a Gwinnett County deputy sheriff discovered he was in the area.

Pugh was convicted of murder earlier this year in Houston County in connection with the 1981 beating death of Mrs. Short's granddaughter,

2-year-old Dana Nicole Mobley, and sentenced to life in prison.

Mrs. Short said her ordeal began 34 days ago, in early December, when she learned Pugh had been set free.

She began a daily effort to see that Pugh was returned to prison.

"The first response I got from DOR was an apology, but they didn't do anything", she said. "I had a hard time getting anything from the state."

But Mrs. Short said state Attorney General Michael Bowers assured her the GBI would try to recapture Pugh.

But it's the Gwinnett County Sheriff's Department that she credits with Pugh's capture.

"They did this for me, because I was having such a hard time getting the state to go after him," she said. "A member of the GBI and the Gwinnett County Sheriff's Department told me they would go after him on their own time if necessary."

"It's hard to think about anyone spending his or her life in prison," she said. "But when you commit a crime, you have to pay. When you love someone like I loved Nikki, there's no limit to your drive. He's caused our families a lot of suffering, and I'm relieved to know he's going back to pay for the hurt he has caused."

All this has been extremely hard for me, but I had to do it for my son. He lived in Warner Robins, GA. And all this had to be done here in Atlanta near where I lived. He would not have had the time off work to spend the hours and days that I did to get this done. It was if I had to get him back for Donny's sake.

The Atlanta Journal calls and asked if they could come to my house to see me on January 10, 1983.

Grandmother keeps at it till slayer found

When Dixie Mobley Short heard that the man who killed her 2 ½ year old granddaughter had been released by mistake from a Wayne County prison, she screamed and she cried. Then she started making telephone calls.

Prison officials and reporters, the governor, lieutenant governor and attorney general all got calls last month from Mrs. Short.

"When you love a grandbaby like I did and have her killed and have the killer escape, you have to do something,: said Mrs. Short. "There is nothing within the law that I would not have done."

Sunday, the phone calls paid off. John Ricky Pugh, who killed Dana Nicole Mobley, was captured in Tennessee on a tip dug up by Georgia Bureau of Investigation officers.

"I got a call from the district attorney down in Houston County, where they tried the case. He told me the squeaking wheel gets the oil and it

was through my effort that Pugh was in custody," Mrs. Short said.

Dressed in lace and black plaid, Mrs. Short talked quietly Sunday about her granddaughter, who was beaten to death in 1981.

"She didn't talk, she just jabbered. She said "daddy" and "flower" and "momo", that's motorcycle."

A dozen pictures of Nikki are scattered about Mrs. Short's home: the child in a rocking chair, wearing a sundress or pink pants, always smiling.

*"At the police station, I picked her up. (*He misunderstood, it was at the funeral home where I had to have her embalmed before they could bring her up to my home town to bury her). *She was just like a rubber doll. Her face was black from the bruises," said Mrs. Short. According to court testimony, the child was beaten to death by Pugh, her mother's boyfriend.*

Mrs. Short said she still was not satisfied that Pugh was released by mistake, or that Georgia officials did all they could to recapture him before she began her prodding. "I'm going to ask the new governor, Joe Frank Harris, for an investigation," she said.

Pugh was released from prison late in November. According to the Department of Offender Rehabilitation. His records showed that he was serving time for a parole violation and that his time was up. The records did not include his murder conviction, a DOR spokesman said.

"They would have captured him eventually, but I truly believe that without my pushing them it could have taken years," Mrs. Short said.

The break, she said, came last month when she met with Attorney General Michael Bowers.

Early indications are that Pugh will fight extradition from Tennessee back to Georgia, said a GBI spokesman.

"I hate to think that anybody has to spend time in prison, but I do feel that he has got to serve whatever time the law requires of him, and I'm glad I was able to do something," Mrs. Short said.

But she wishes that she could have done more to prevent the killing rather than see the killer punished. "We tried to get custody of the child, but we couldn't."

...Yes, I have some guilt feelings. I did all I could at the time, but I wish there was more I had done."

Turning quickly from a photograph of her granddaughter, Mrs. Short points to a bedroom wall.

"Right through that wall is the cemetery where she's buried, Eternal Hills. I take her a rose every month, on the seventh, when she was murdered."

"I took her one Friday, I'll do it until I die, if possible", she said.

There were more Newspaper Clippings about the capture, mostly saying the same things.

Another one:

Busbee Given Paper Seeking Pugh's Return

From Perry, GA. Houston County District Attorney Theron Finlayson Monday hand-delivered to Gov. George Busbee extradition papers for the return to Houston County of convicted killer John Ricky Pugh.

Finlayson intends to file escape charges against Pugh, who was captured Sunday in Tennessee after being accidentally released from Georgia's prison system.

"We hope to apprehend him in a few days," Finlayson said in a statement read to reporters after he departed for Atlanta to deliver the extradition papers. 'We hope to have him back in Houston County in a few days."

Vicki Snow, an employee in the governor's office who handles extradition proceedings, said Finlayson delivered the papers about 5 pm. She said the fact that Joe Frank Harris replaces Busbee today will not jeopardize the extradition request.

Pugh, 29, convicted of the 1981 murder of a 2-year-old girl, is being held in Loudon, Tenn., where he was taken into custody. Pugh has indicated he will fight extradition to Georgia.

Pugh was released Nov. 23 from the Wayne County Correctional Institution in what was described as a paperwork mix-up. He had served less than a year following his Feb. 23, 1982 conviction by a Houston County jury for the beating death of Dana Nicole Mobley.

Authorities were unaware of Pugh's release from the prison by Department of Offender Rehabilitation officials until he called the child's mother.

The Gwinnett County Sheriff's Department became involved in the investigation after the victim's grandmother, Dixie Mobley Short, began a single-handed campaign from her Snellville home to seek Pugh's recapture.

Gwinnett deputies called Mrs. Short Saturday to say they were preparing to go to Tennessee for Pugh's arrest. One of the Gwinnett officials involved in the search, Deputy Sheriff Willard Baxter, told Mrs. Short he got involved after he read newspaper accounts of her effort to have Pugh recaptured.

Mrs. Short said Finlayson called her Sunday and said her determination to get state officials to admit an error in Pugh's release helped in the recapture.

Mrs. Short said she also received a call Sunday from Georgia Attorney General Mike Bowers notifying her of Pugh's arrest. Mrs. Short met with Bowers in December to urge state officials to step up their search for Pugh.

Pugh was released after he completed a sentence on another charge, DOR officials said they had no record of his murder conviction.

Even though he was released, Finlayson said he considers Pugh an escapee because he knew his release was accidental.

Convicted Child Killer Is Back In Custody

Houston County officials were to begin extradition procedures today to return John Ricky Pugh — the convicted child murderer who was accidentally released from a Wayne County prison facility Nov. 23 — to Georgia.

Pugh was recaptured in Loudon, Tenn., Sunday by the Loudon County Sheriff's Department, following an investigation by officers of the Georgia Bureau of Investigation and the Gwinnett County Sheriff's Department.

Pugh had been convicted of the Feb. 8, 1981, stomping death of 2-year-old Dana Nicole Mobley, his former girlfriend's child, and sentenced to life in prison. An apparent paperwork error led to his release.

According to GBI agent Jimmy Davis, Pugh was recaptured without incident Sunday morning when he was surprised by sheriff's deputies in the southern Tennessee town, located just north of Chattanooga. Pugh had reportedly been hiding out with acquaintances, after having been taken to Tennessee by his mother.

The Atlanta metro fugitive squad involved with the investigation, which began in Mobile, Ala., where Pugh's mother reportedly lives.

Davis said much of the credit for the investigation belonged to Gwinnett County Deputy Sheriff Willard Baxter, who is a member of the fugitive squad and who discovered some of the leads that guided the investigation through Alabama and Tennessee.

Baxter and Jack Hamilton, chief deputy of the Gwinnett County Sheriff's Department, became involved in the Pugh case after reading a newspaper article about a Snellville woman's fight to get her granddaughter's murderer behind bars.

Dixie Mobley Short, Dana Nicole's paternal grandmother, had learned of Pugh's accidental release on Dec. 6, after the freed convict called the murdered child's mother to tell her he was free.

Short became angry when she learned that the mistake was due to a paperwork mix-up and that the state apparently was dragging its heels with the investigation.

In an interview following Pugh's release, Short had said the entire incident was a case of "professional buck-passing."

Intent on getting Pugh back in prison, Short began a process of drawing attention to the case, though the use of the media and through personal contacts with state officials. With the help of state Rep. Mike Barnett, Short said, she talked to several officials, including state Attorney General Michael Bowers.

At the time, Short had said that her goals were to get Pugh back in prison, to find out why the error happened, where it happened, and what the state would do to correct it.

"I will get my answer," she had said. 'If I have to, I'll go the Washington. If I have to, I'll stand on the street corner with a cup and beg for money to get to Washington. "

According to Baxter, his interest in the case was partly fueled by the actions of Short. He said he had "a special desire to see Pugh caught because of the family. The grandmother is s fine lady and she has gone about this thing the right way. "

Baxter and Hamilton visited Short in her home in mid-December, and the investigation proceeded from there.

"They said they felt I should not have to go through what I was going through," Short said. "They said they would take it (the case) on if the state didn't. They told me, we don't want to build your hopes up, but we haven't gone after a man yet we didn't catch. "

According to Hamilton, the case was a personal responsibility.

"If the system fails, we have all failed. All of us in law enforcement have a responsibility," he said.

"We planned to locate him if it meant taking time off ourselves," he said.

On Wednesday, Jan. 5, Baxter called Short, telling her that he had an official warrant for Pugh's arrest and that his bags were packed.

Thirty-four days after she started her campaign to get Pugh recaptured, on Sunday morning at 10 a.m.

Short received a phone call from Debra Mobley, Nikki's mother, telling her that the man was in custody. Later in the morning, Attorney General Bowers called her to confirm the news.

"I was just shocked," she said. "You were hoping and hoping, but when you get the phone call, you are shocked."

Following what she called a 34-day non-stop nightmare," Short said the phone calls seemed to lift the "weight of the world off my shoulders."

Short said that she does think the investigation would not have taken place as quickly as it did if she had not pressed the issue.

"The D.A. from Warner Robbins (Theron Finlayson) called. He said the squeaky wheel gets the oil. He thanked me. He said through my drive and assistance and determination, they got him."

"I've been labeled the angry grandmother from Snellville," she said, "but I got what I went after."

The second anniversary of Nikki's death is coming in a few months, Short said, and while Pugh may be in custody, all of her questions have not been answered.

Recapture Didn't End Her Quest

When some bureaucrats in state government have a bad dream at night, Dixie Mobley Short may be in it.

Dixie Mobley Short, the grandmother-turned-whistle blower on bureaucratic ineptitude, has given new meaning to persistence and made state officials beware.

Thirty-four days after she started a single-handed campaign to draw attention to the bungling of prison records that allowed the release of a convicted murderer serving a life sentence for the slaying of her 2-year-old granddaughter, Mrs. Short got the thing she wanted most — his recapture.

And the return of John Ricky Pugh to Georgia last week was largely the result of Mrs. Short's mettle.

But Mrs. Short, who spent hundreds of hours on the phone to state officials, investigators and reporters trying to piece together what happened and how state officials handled it, isn't through.

She has requested — and the commissioner of the Department of Offender Rehabilitation has personally said he will comply — an internal report explaining what allowed the mistake and who was to blame.

For the 34 days between Nov. 24, 1982, when Pugh was released, and Jan. 9, when a sleepy rural postman in Tennessee led lawmen to the residence where Pugh was staying. Mrs. Short let nobody — not even the news media — forget she expected answers.

With Pugh's return to Houston County, where he was convicted in February 1982 for the stomping death of Dana Nicole Mobley, Mrs. Short has disproved cynics who pooh-poohed her persistence.

What the 46 year-old woman did was draw so much attention to the accidentally release of Pugh that sympathetic law enforcement officers set out on their own time and captured Pugh.

"We have really suffered, I didn't sleep, I hurt, and my family hurt for me," said Mrs. Short in an interview recently from her Gwinnett County home.

"It's taught me that people have got to become involved," she said. "It would have been easy to sit back, but I saw the state wasn't going to do anything but try and buy time."

When she began calling state officials to find out what error allowed the release of Pugh from the Wayne County Correctional Institution, Mrs. Short quickly encountered what she described as "monumental, professional buck-passing."

"They were too busy trying to blame things on Houston County,", she said. Originally the Department of Offender Rehabilitation, which administers Georgia's prison system, placed the blame for Pugh's release on court officials in Houston County where Pugh had been tried.

DOR officials initially said they had not been notified about the life sentence, which allowed Pugh's release after completion of a sentence for a parole violation.

Later, the DOR said someone had erroneously placed "Clayton County" on records to show where Pugh had been convicted. Officials said they checked in Clayton County and when authorities there said they knew nothing of Pugh's conviction, he was released. Moreover, because Pugh had not escaped, DOR officials said they were not obliged to launch a search.

Mrs. Short set to work that day, calling DOR officials, local lawmakers and court officials in Houston County where her son and ex-daughter-in-law still live.

"At night I would make a list of people I would call. Then I'd get up and make as many as I could before I left for work at 8:30," she said. Coming home for lunch from her job as a secretary at a real estate firm, she made more calls.

"At one point I added them up and there were 100 people I had contacted. I don't know exactly how many it was though. It has been tough for my family, we've gone through so much agony, but they've been very understanding.

Among those she talked or met with was Attorney General Mike Bowers, who asked she keep him briefed. After a story about Mrs. Short's plight appeared in the Gwinnett County News, she was approached by Gwinnett County Sheriff Willard Baxter and Chief Deputy Jack Hamilton.

"At the time I wasn't getting anywhere and they said they were concerned about my drive. They offered to work on locating Pugh on their own time. I checked with Bowers and he opened a case and they assigned a GBI agent."

The lawmen first went to Alabama and then the small Tennessee town of Loudon, where Pugh had been taken to a relative's home. Pugh, 29, was arrested without incident.

"Mr. Baxter called me up one night and said, "I've got my bags packed and leaving in the morning to get your man."

"On a Sunday morning, I'll never forget, Debra called me and told me he had been caught. All I could do was give a big sigh of relief."

Mrs. Short said she still is awaiting the DOR report and intends to write a book about the ordeal.

"It's such a relief. If I hadn't done this I would have destroyed myself because I've still got a son down in Houston County, she said." The son, divorced from Nikki's mother, was the father of the child.

Dixie Short helped generate a lot of news articles after the murder of her grandchild "Nikki"

Persistence pays off in recapture of child's killer

When Dixie Mobley Short heard that the man who killed her 2 ½ year-old granddaughter had been released by mistake from a Wayne County prison, she screamed and she cried. Then she started making telephone calls.

Prison officials and reporters, the governor, lieutenant governor and attorney general all got calls last month from Mrs. Short.

"When you love a grandbaby like I did and have her killed and have the killer escape, you have to do something", said Mrs. Short. "There is nothing within the law that I would not have done."

Sunday, the phone calls paid off. John Ricky Pugh, who killed Dana Nicole Mobley, was captured in Tennessee on a tip dug up by Georgia Bureau of Investigation officers.

"I got a call from the district attorney down in Houston County, where they tried the case. He told me the squeaking wheel gets the oil and it was through my effort that Pugh was in custody," Mrs. Short said.

Dressed in lace and black plaid, Mrs. Short talked quietly Sunday about her granddaughter, who was beaten to death in 1981.

"She didn't talk, she just jabbered. She said 'daddy' and 'flower' and 'momo' — that's motorcycle."

140

A dozen pictures of "Nikki" are scattered about Mrs. Short's home: the child in a rocking chair, wearing a sundress or pink pants, always smiling. "At the police station I picked her up. She was just like a rubber doll. Her face was black from the bruises," said Mrs. Short. (Actually it was not the police station where I picked her up and held her, it was at the morgue in Warner Robins.) *According to court testimony, the child was beaten to death by Pugh, her mother's boyfriend.*

Mrs. Short said she still was not satisfied that Pugh was released by mistake, or that Georgia officials did all they could to recapture him before she began her prodding. "I'm going to ask the new governor, Joe Frank Harris, for an investigation" she said.

Pugh was released from prison late in November. According to the Department of Offender Rehabilitation, his records showed that he was serving time for a parole violation and that his time was up. The records did not include his murder conviction, said DOR.

"They would have captured him eventually, but I truly believe that without my pushing them it could have taken years," Mrs. Short said.

The break, she said, came late last month when she met with Attorney General Michael Bowers. Early indications are that Pugh will fight extradition from Tennessee back to Georgia, said a GBI spokesman.

"I hate to think that anybody has to spend time in prison, but I do feel that he has got to serve

whatever time the law requires of him, and I'm glad I was able to do something," said Mrs. Short. But she wishes that she could have done more to prevent the murder rather than see the killer punished. "We tried to get custody of the child, but we couldn't.

....Yes, I have some guilt feelings. I did all I could at the time, but I wish there was more I had done.

Turning quickly from a photograph of her granddaughter, Mrs. Short points to a bedroom wall.

"Right through that wall is the cemetery where she's buried, Eternal Hills. I take her a rose every month on the seventh, when she was murdered.

"I took her one Friday. I'll do it until I die," she said.

Unfortunately, I had to stop going every month after many years as I went to work before daylight, and did not get home until after dark. Still go on birthdays, anniversaries, Easter, Christmas, etc. and times in between.

We waited and waited until almost 30- days had passed. I had heard that if not extradited within 30 days that Tennessee would have to release him. I knew we could not go through that again.

Just before the 30 days were up, I made an appointment to visit Mr. Peters at the Department of Rehilibation. I was so upset. I told him if he did not get Pugh back to Georgia before Tennessee had to release him, if he did not think I pitched a fit the first time, just wait until the 2nd time. I told him I would climb on the top of the State Capital and tell the world what they were doing. He looked me straight in the eyes and said, "I know you will."

The Attorney General called me at work the next day and told me they were on their way back to Georgia with Pugh, and where did I want him. I told him I would like to see Pugh placed in Reidsville. At least there seemed to be more security there than the small county prisons.

Compassion and Justice:

Macon Telegraph & News: *Child-murderer John Ricky Pugh should never have been released from the Wayne County Correctional Institution. It was a colossal mix-up in the state's penal system, for which Department of Rehabillitation officials apologized to the victim's distraught grandmother, Dixie Short of Snellville.*

The matter might have ended there, but for Mrs. Short's determination. She began a daily effort to see that Pugh served out his sentence for the 1981 beating death of two-year-old Dana Nicole Mobley in Houston County.

She lucked out. An agent of the Georgia Bureau of Investigation got involved. At about the same time, a member of the Gwinnett County Sheriff's Department, whose only connection was that he had read about the DOR goof in the newspapers, volunteered to help. The two men told her they would go after Pugh — on their own time, if necessary.

Together they went to Mobile, Alabama, (Pugh's home-town) and developed leads that led them to Loudon, Tenn., where local officials arrested Pugh Sunday. He has refused to return voluntarily to Georgia.

That puts the problem back in the lap of Houston officials, who are at least partly to blame for the record-keeping foul-up that led to Pugh's illegitimate release. Houston District Attorney Theron Finlayson is presumably working on extradition proceedings.

But if justice is done, it will be because of the determination of a heart-broken grandmother and the compassion of two law enforcement officers, whose names we don't know. We commend them.

Chapter Nineteen

Well, he is in Reidsville and I am hoping everything will settle down now. Then I received some disturbing news.

Debbie sent me a lot of paperwork regarding Davy. A lot of it was very disturbing.

It seemed that a new attorney for Pugh visited Davy at the prison. He stated that he and a friend had gone to Pugh's apartment to get Pugh to go purchase some liquor for them.

Isn't it ironic that the friend's father was a Judge?

Davy mentioned Pugh and the friend were only gone 15 minutes. He also talked about a wrestling match killing Nikki, but would not elaborate in any sense at all on what he meant by a wrestling match. He also mentioned that someone had fallen on Nikki and would not tell him who this person was, or how he even knew that someone had fallen on Nikki.

When asked about his religion, he told the attorney that he became involved in the worship of the devil.

This gets me to thinking, could Davy have had anything to do with her death? Is Ricky Pugh the real guilty person?

I called the District Attorney, Theron Finlayson and expressed my concern. I received this letter from him.

Dear Mrs. Short:

I have been informed of your desire for information concerning the prosecution of John Ricky Pugh. Mr. Pugh was convicted in a jury trial in which he was represented by counsel and I would point out that Mr. Pugh testified in his own behalf. In addition, his conviction was upheld on appeal to the Georgia Supreme Court.

As recently as three months ago I testified in a Habeas Corpus hearing in which Mr. Pugh was represented by new attorneys. It is my strong belief that Mr. Pugh is guilty of murder, as has been reflected by his conviction and appeals, and I would not want it on my conscience to have convicted an innocent man. This office will always pursue any new evidence along these lines; however, I have found no evidence suggesting that any other individual perpetrated this crime. Rest assured that we will remain unfailing in our resolve should competent evidence arise.

If I can be of further assistance, or answer any questions, please feel free to let me know. With best regards, I am Theron Finlayson

Now, knowing myself very well, I feel the need to get to the bottom of this.

While sitting at my desk at work, it came to me that I needed to go to the prison and question Pugh about leaving Davy alone with Nikki. (Recently I re-read the transcript from the trial and there was definitely no mention of Davy left alone with Nikki.)

I also knew that I had to put as much of this behind me before I could get on with my life. There comes a time when you have to "just let go," or you become a very bitter person.

I do not know if "forgiving" is the right word, but I knew I could not go on forever with hatred in my heart, and now he would serve the time the state sentenced him to serve.

I wrote to the prison to get permission to come down to Reidsville, and to be sure Pugh would talk to me if I went down.

After several letters back and forth, I received approval. Now whom can I get to go with me. My sister Connie came to mind that would be crazy enough to go with me on my trip.

I called her and she agreed to go. I told her we would leave on Saturday, stay in a nice motel, and have a good meal that night and I would go to the prison early on Sunday and we could head back home later that afternoon.

Connie and I packed our overnight bags and left her house around 4 PM. We had originally planned to drive just past Macon and stop for the night.

On our way, we were eyewitnesses to an automobile accident. Connie said, "Only a thing like this could happen to you." We saw that the woman that caused the accident was not going to stop. Also, there were other cars stopping so we decided to go after the woman that caused the accident. We chased the car and got the tag number of the person driving that had caused the accident and went back to the scene. The woman was going at a high rate of speed and we finally caught up with her when we reached the interstate where she had to slow down for other traffic. The injured parties thanked us, and after explaining to the police what we had seen, we decided to continue our trip to Reidsville.

As we reached Macon, the sun was still shinning, so we decided to drive on until dark, then we would not have so much driving on Sunday morning and we would get to the prison early, and get an early start back.

After we passed Macon, there was nothing on the Interstate. I believe we passed one or two service stations, but none of the signs mentioned anything about lodging. There was nothing else to do but drive on. We reached the exit, and asked how far it was on to Reidsville. Since it was only 20 miles away, and just barely dark, we decided to risk going on. When we arrived in Reidsville, we saw a small motel on the main street, named "Dixie Motel."

Surely there would be a nicer one around close. We were hoping for at least a Holiday Inn, there we were just going to take a bath, get something to eat and just enjoy the night in luxury, (we thought). We stopped and asked about the Motels and found that was the only one in the town, and there was not another one anywhere nearby.

We went into the motel Office and registered. The clerk was telling us something about someone committing suicide, and his brother was at Reidsville. I was trying so hard not to listen, as I just did not want anything else to have to think about that night.

When we got to our room and turned on the lights, I wondered if we could get a refund on this place. Roaches ran everywhere, the glass panels had been broken on the door, and Connie said, "Remember that was what the lady was telling us about this room." The mirror on the dresser was broken in half. There was nothing we could do but try to stay here and make the best of it, or sleep in the car. We checked our beds, and they seemed to be clean. We left the room and went out to look for something to eat.

We found one small restaurant to get a hamburger. There were no nice restaurants anywhere. We could barely eat thinking of our room to which we had to go back. We decided to drive around the small town before going back to the Motel. The whole place was becoming more and more depressing. I wondered a couple times if this was the thing for me to do, and I decided that if God had led me here to talk with Pugh, then I would make the best of it.

We went back to the room, and it was only 9 PM. We decided to take our bath and watch TV for a while and get up early to get to the prison for the 8 AM visiting hours and then get out of this place as fast as we could.

Just as I got into the shower and pulled the curtain, roaches jumped down and joined me. I took a shoe to bed with me to kill the bugs that climbed up the wall beside me. Would this night ever end? I do not believe I slept over one hour all total that night.

We found a place to eat breakfast, or eat at breakfast. We seemed to have lost our appetite by now.

I arrived at the prison just around 8 AM, and drove to the microphone to where the sign told me to go. I explained to the woman up in the tower who I was and who I was to see there. She told me to park and go in the gate.

Inside, I filled out some papers explaining that I had mailed the necessary paperwork, and received prior approval by both the prison and Pugh to come down today.

She explained that this approval was just for today only. I said I was glad, because I did not believe I would never want to come back to this place. Inside they run a gadget over my entire body before letting me into a room with about 50 groups of chairs in groups of four each. After waiting 30 minutes or so, Pugh entered the room.

I did not know what his reaction would be when seeing me even though he had approved of my visit.

I had inquired if I could bring him a Bible, but apparently, he had one.

I explained to him that I had received some papers that his attorney had written after visiting with Davy. I wanted to hear first hand from him what took place that afternoon, and why he did not mention in the trial that Davy had been to the apartment that afternoon.

Not one word at the trial indicated leaving Davy there alone with Nikki that Saturday afternoon. I asked him if he had told his attorney about this before the trial. He said he had; I asked why there was no mention of it at the trial.

When he answered most of my questions, I left the prison to head for home.

I did not feel as though I got the answers I wanted, so when I got back home, I called his first attorney and asked him if Pugh had told him he left Davy there alone with her.

He said no, Pugh had not, yet Davy talked with Pugh's new attorney about being there.

Pugh was still guilty of leaving this young man there with a two- year- old child.

Now, I have to live the rest of my life wondering.......

God was not finished with me just yet. I had a very serious surgery. After being in the intensive care unit for a while, I was placed in a room. I was going to be released on the tenth day, but unfortunately, on the ninth day I developed a blood clot in my lung at which I almost died. I did not see the light at the end of the tunnel as some often mentions, but I remember feeling completely at peace after the initial pain.

Now I know why God kept me here on this earth for a while. There was another cross I had to bear.

As if burying one grandchild was not bad enough, I was about to bury the second grandchild, both who died by the hands of another in a terrible way.

No farewell words were spoken,
No time to say good-bye,
You were gone before we knew it,
And only God knows why.
unknown

This applies to all three of my grandchildren.

My second son Rick and his wife Karen had a baby girl in 1989 that was still born. We were all very saddened about this.

Foreword

Randy Mobley

I have always felt like I had a pretty good childhood. My dad was in the Air Force, so we moved around a little when I was growing up, but not excessively. My first memories are of us living in Newfoundland, Canada, where we lived until I was 5 or 6 years old. I remember fun times riding sleds and toboggans and digging snow caves. Next we moved to Cheyenne, Wyoming. Here I accumulated more great memories of horse back riding, going to rodeos, and camping somewhere in the Rocky Mountains. After that we moved to Richmond, Virginia, and then Warner Robins, Georgia. My parents divorced when I was about 13 years old. I didn't really understand all of the reasons…but even though our family split, things weren't too bad for me. Since I was the only child young enough for my Dad to get for weekend visitations, I got to spend a lot of one on one time with him. He took me fishing and skeet shooting, and several trips to Panama City where we would go out on the deep-sea fishing boats out of Captain Anderson's Pier. In addition to the time alone spent with Dad, I also gained the best stepfather you could ask for, Henry Short. Mom and Henry moved us to the Atlanta area, and although I wasn't too thrilled with leaving my friends at the time, I soon met new friends and the opportunities living closer to Atlanta were an improvement over Warner Robins. I graduated from South Gwinnett High School, and later got an Associates Degree in Electronics from Dekalb Community College.

We were a Christian family, and while I have always believed in God, we were somewhat sporadic regarding church attendance. I remember my parents taking me to church, but I don't recall ever really getting involved or becoming a member of a church.

Life started to get harder while I was in high school. My father was diagnosed with a brain tumor and was dead within a month. Then, while I was in college my 2-year-old niece, my ex-sister-in-laws ex-con boyfriend killed Nikki. That was the kind of tragedy that only happened on TV…I'm not sure if it ever really hit me how tragic that was for Mom, Donny and Nikki's mom, Debbie (at least not until much later in my life). Then I was in a severe motorcycle accident where I almost lost my life and my leg. It took me almost 2 years to recover to the point where I didn't require a cast, crutch, or brace of some kind to walk. My mom quit work so that she could help take care of me during this time, and that was a huge blessing. I graduated from college and landed a great job at Rockwell International's Missile Systems, where I met my first wife, Cindy, and the mother of my children. We had two wonderful children, Krista and Jamie. Cindy was diabetic, and she greatly rebelled again her disease, refusing to follow medical advice regarding, diet, exercise, and smoking. As her medical condition worsened, so did our marriage. After a bitter divorce, I was awarded custody of our children, who were only about 1 ½ and 3 years old at the time. A year and half later, Cindy passed away from kidney failure, which stemmed from her diabetes and other related health issues. So there I was, a single parent of two young children at the age of 30.

I have so many great memories of raising Krista and Jamie. Being a single parent, I was very close to my children, and we did everything together. We went camping and hiking together. I bought a boat and taught the kids to ski and ride a kneeboard. We started a twice-yearly camping trip at Lake Harwell with good friends that became a 15-year tradition. We learned to snow ski and later to snowboard. We took karate together, and Krista and Jamie earned their red belts, while I only progressed as far as a purple belt. So as great as things were, I was terribly lonely and depressed. I did not like being single, and not many women were interested in dating a guy with two young children. The women I did date always turned out to have a lot of baggage of their own. During this time I came to believe that God did not really care about me. I believed in his existence, but I did not believe that he took any interest in our day- to-day lives. That changed when I met my current wife, Teri. We had known each other a few years as coworkers, but she was married so even thought I was attracted to her, she was unavailable and I never gave much thought to dating her.

Time passed, and Teri divorced, and we started dating. For me, it became obvious pretty quickly that she was my soul mate, as we had so much in common. My faith was strengthened, as marrying Teri was the answer to my prayers. We dated a year, and after I proposed we were engaged for a year, and then we were married. Krista and Jamie were 13 and 11 years old when we married. Things did not necessarily go smoothly at first. We had issues that are probably typical of a blended family, learning to respect each other and put up with each other. Teri got us all back into going to church regularly, and we became members of Hamilton Mill Methodist Church. It was a bit of a struggle getting the kids to attend, but gradually they came to like it, or at least accept it. We wouldn't find out until later how important that was. My faith was tested about 5 years later.

January 17th, 2005 was Martin Luther King's birthday, and the kids were out of school. We had intended to make Jamie go spend the day at my mom's, but he wanted to sleep in and hang out with his friends in the neighborhood, and we felt bad making him go to his grand mom's, so we let him stay home. I got a call at work around 4pm. It was a female police officer, she was at our house, and she said that someone had been shot. I was somewhat in disbelief, but I grabbed Teri and we started home as fast as we could. We didn't know what to think…I had guns in the house, but they were in a locked gun case under our bed, and we kept our bedroom door locked as well. I had installed a deadbolt on our bedroom door, and we kept it locked anytime we were away from home, as we were concerned about the kids having friends over (even though it was forbidden for them to have company in the house when we weren't home). On the way, we finally got hold of my mom, who was at our house and crying hysterically. She said that Jamie had been shot and taken to the hospital. We rushed to the hospital, where we learned that Jamie had been shot in the neck, severing his carotid artery, and the wound was deemed fatal.

I spent the next day and a half at Jamie's bedside. I pleaded with him to hang on, and I prayed and pleaded with God to save my son's life. Our associate pastor, David Whitworth, stayed overnight at the hospital with us, trying to offer what support he could. Sometime in the middle of the night, as I sat holding Jamie's hand, David placed his hand on my back. I felt God's strength flow thru him and into me. I understood then that it was not God's will for Jamie to live, and if he did he would be mentally and physically crippled forever. I told Jamie then that it was OK if he had to go, that I was proud of him and loved him so much, but it was OK. Jamie moved his hand slightly, and that was the last time that I saw any sign of consciousness in him. We stayed at the hospital until the evening of January 18th, when the doctors pronounced Jamie brain dead. Jamie had opted to be an organ donor when he had acquired his learner's permit, so he was kept on machine's to keep his organ's alive even though he was gone. It was so hard to leave the hospital that night. Jamie appeared to be physically alive, but I knew that he was gone.

The following weeks and months were so hard. I now knew what my Mom and brother had gone thru after Nikki's death. God gave me the strength to get thru that night, and he taught me forgiveness. I knew then that Jamie's friend, who had been holding the gun when it fired, would continue to suffer for years if not forever. Teri and I reached out to him and his family. We made sure that they knew we didn't blame them for Jamie's death, and that they were welcome at his funeral.

Going thru Jamie's belongings we found some of his writings, where he talked about his faith in God. We knew then that Jamie was in heaven, that we would see him again some day, and that helped us to carry on. I don't know how those without faith can survive life's tragedies.

It took many years for us to recover from Jamie's loss, and we have learned so much. We now know that although you can never "get over" the loss of a loved one, you can heal and carry on. We know that while God does not answer the question "why", he does give us the strength to survive life's tragedies. Life has gone on, and while we think about Jamie all the time, Teri and I have found happiness for now. I know that there will be more losses someday. We are all destined to lose everyone we love eventually, but if we keep faith in God, he will get us thru it, until we all meet again in Heaven.

Chapter One

Today is Martin Luther King Jr.'s birthday holiday. I was lying in bed with a headache, talking on the phone with my sister Connie. We were discussing that some days we just wait for the next bombshell to drop on us. About that time, I told her Randy was beeping in and I needed to take his call. He said, "Mom, a neighbor just called and said Police were all over my yard and would I go over to see what was going on?" I think he knew more than he was telling me, but did not want to alarm me.

I jumped out of bed, not even combing my hair, and rushed out the door to go over to Randy's house. Little did I know the television cameras would soon be in my face. I did not go over to get Jamie that day as I usually did because Krista, his older sister was home, and it was such a beautiful day, I thought I would just let him stay home and play for the day. Randy had already told me he slept in until late morning. I called him around lunch and he was fine.

I called Jamie's house from my cell phone on the way to see what was going on. A police officer answered the phone. I told her who I was and I asked her what was going on. She told me a young man named James had been shot and for me to get over there as fast as I could, but drive careful. I just started screaming and screamed all the way over his house. When I turned into the subdivision, I saw all the television helicopters flying above, and people were standing all up and down the street. I drove up as far as I could go and got out of the car. I went up to a police officer, told him I was the grandmother, and asked what happened. I was terrified after seeing all that was going on, and shaking all over, terrified of what the officer would say.

He told me a boy shot Jamie. I looked in their police car and recognized the young boy sitting in the car. I did not ask many questions then, just wanted to know where Jamie was. They told me the ambulance had already taken him to the hospital. I asked a neighbor if a sheet was over his face and she said it was not, so I assumed he was still alive.

The boy that shot him ran over to a neighbor who was a nurse to try to get help. He said Jamie told him to call 911.

In the meantime, I talked with Randy and Teri, Jamie's parents, and they were on their way to the hospital and they asked me if I would stay there to wait for Krista, and come on to the hospital.

Still not knowing what had happened, when the media kept asking me questions, I told them that Randy always kept his guns locked, and they were in their bedroom and I knew they had always kept the bedroom door locked.

A couple of times when I would hear about a young person shot and killed by a gun, I would ask Randy again where his guns were. He always told me they were locked in a safe.

After what seemed a long time, Krista came home from the mall, and we went to the hospital. I kept thinking is injuries were in the arm or leg, and they could help him.

When we got to the hospital, Teri told me it was very serious. I had called my husband Henry, and my son Donny. They were already there. Many people were already gathering outside the intensive care unit. I had called Marilyn, a friend from my Sunday school class and asked her to call the group and ask them to pray for Jamie. Many of the women had already arrived at the hospital. They had already seen the accident on the news.

Rick, Karen and their families arrived from Alabama as well as Jamie's maternal grandmother. Karen's parents came to help them with the children during the funeral. Two Pastors from Jamie's church were there. One stayed with us the entire time.

Randy sat by Jamie's bed and did not leave it except to go to the rest room and then he literally ran there and back. He and Teri did not eat or leave the room but for a moment all night or the next day.

I went in to see Jamie and knew just how serious it was. I kissed him on the cheek and told him I could kiss him all I wanted to now and he could not stop me. A tear ran down his face. He was at the age he would barely allow me to kiss him.

We all planned to stay the night at the hospital. During the night, I remembered the police had the front door open in Randy and Teri's house, and I was concerned that Teri and Krista's cat would get out, as they never went outside. The police would not allow me to go in the house before I left for the hospital as they were still investigating. They had the yellow crime tape all around the house and yard.

Donny and I decided to go over to the house after midnight to check on the animals and the house and to lock it up. It took a while to find Teri's cat, but Krista's was up in the cat tree in her room, both traumatized with the shooting, and police officers all over the house.

During the time at Jamie's bedside Randy kept saying he just knew the police would come to arrest him when he found out the boys had gotten into his bedroom and figured out the combination on the gun case.

The police officers did come by the hospital to check on Jamie and I asked them if they were going to arrest Randy. I told them he was so worried about that. He wanted to stay every minute with Jamie. They told me they were not going to arrest him as he had done everything right by having the case locked and the bedroom door locked. Two fifteen-year-old boys figured out how to get both of them open.

Henry had just put a cat door in their bedroom door and the boys somehow got something through it to open the lock, and then got the gun case open. They were just playing "dry shoot" with the guns. Only one of the guns was loaded, and his friend had it. He unloaded the bullets on the bed and began playing with it. It seems one bullet had "dropped down in the chamber" and that bullet hit Jamie in the neck. Jamie knew gun safety so well. I was surprised about that. One of his friends said they had a conversation just recently where one friend said the gun was not loaded and Jamie said, "You treat every gun as if it were loaded."

I think the X-Box game they had been playing so often got them to go into the bedroom and get the real guns to play with.

Randy had taken Jamie out to shoot the guns several times, to be sure he knew safety.

It became obvious that Jamie was not going to live after they did tests the following afternoon and told us that he was brain dead.

When Jamie had gotten his learners license a few months earlier, he put on the back that he would like to be an organ donor.

Randy and Teri started arranging for the donation of his undamaged organs.

I am still holding out hope that he will live. I prayed that if God would let him live that I would take care of him. I even tried to "bargain" with God. That was not in God's plan. Randy told me that if Jamie would have lived, that he would not have any kind of life and would see his friends outside playing and him in a wheel chair or in bed all the time.

Not all this sank in to me. I think I was in such shock and disbelief that I did not understand all that was going on. I just felt numb and going through the motions.

Later on during the early morning hours, almost everyone had gone home except the immediate family and a cousin of mine, Glyndia. She kept asking me if I wanted her to comb my hair. I remembered I did not comb it before I left home. I was in such a hurry to go see about Jamie, I did not care what I looked like. Heaven only knows what I looked like when the news media had the cameras on me. Frankly, I did not care. I only wanted Jamie to live.

Sitting there in the wee hours, I started thinking about Jamie and Krista.

Krista had always spent many weekends with us, and Jamie started staying with us on weekends when he was just a few months old. Jamie was born pre-mature and stayed in the neonatal unit for a while.

I took Krista to church with me on Sunday mornings. She was always dressed like a living doll.

One Sunday morning when Jamie was two months old, I decided not to go to church that day. I had not read the newspaper that morning as I usually did. I had been up all night trying to find my brother and sister-in-law in California. The earthquake of 1989 at the Golden Gate Bridge had happened that weekend and we had not heard from them. They lived right in the area.

My mother lived in the apartment that Henry built on our house for her. She was so worried about them.

Later on in the afternoon, my sister and her husband came over. Henry was cooking dinner for us, and I was reading the paper.

My brother Shorty lived in a building out back of our house. He had a brain tumor and I had taken care of him for the last five years. He was an alcoholic and I did not want him in the house with us. He had a very comfortable place to live, heated and had a TV in his room.

I noticed he had not come home the night before, but often he stayed with whomever he would meet up with and come home later.

On the front page of the paper, it read about an unidentified man run over on highway 78 in Loganville. The more I read, the more I became so afraid it was my brother. It described a blue plaid coat and black boots. I told my sister I was afraid it was "Shorty," his nickname. I called the number in the paper and talked with a woman at the police station. She asked me how old my brother was and I told her he was 54 years old. She said it could not be him because the deceased man was much younger judging from the muscles of his body.

I still was not satisfied, and my sister asked why we did not go out to his place and see if his coat was there. It was not.

I came back in the house, called the number again, and told the woman that the description sounded too much like my brother. Then she asked me, "Was my brother missing any fingers?" I knew then it was indeed Shorty. He had lost two of his fingers working on a car several years earlier.

We told her we did not want the police to come to our house to discuss the accident, as it would upset my mother too much. We had to find a way to tell her. Betty, Donald, Henry, and I left to go to a place nearby to talk with them. We just cut the stove off and left. Randy had already picked up the children.

When we met with the police all we had to identify him by was a picture of his arm that had a bluebird tattoo on it. Also, they matched fingerprints. Seven cars ran over him, and there was not anything left to identify but the arm.

We called the rest of our brothers and sisters and asked them to come to my house, but wait in the road out in front until we got there.

Mother had come over to our side and saw that we had just cut off the stove and left. When she saw all the cars coming in the driveway, she came running out thinking we had heard news that our brother died in the earthquake.

Shorty's death was very, very hard on me. I had done my best to look after him for five years.

Later after the funeral, we heard from my other brother that was in the earthquake. They had walked down to see all the damage, and could not go back to their house. My sister-in-law had left her elderly mother in their house. They got one of the police to go up to their house, get one of their cars, and get the mother to bring to them. They went to a nearby town and got a Motel room.

The next week I drove down to the place where Shorty died. I also drove beyond it at the exact time of the accident to see if in fact you could see him in the road. I could not. I traced his actions that entire day. Visited everyone I heard he had visited to see if I could find out anything. Did he stand in the fast lane on purpose, or did he think he was in the turn lane?

I think the first two cars stopped, but none of the other seven stopped. They probably thought by then it was just an animal as there was nothing to see. They scooped up his remains with a shovel and put it in a bucket.

A schoolgirl drove the second car. I had heard she was having a hard time with the fact she had run over him, and I asked her parents if I could talk with her.

I convinced her that her hitting him was unavoidable. She told my cousin in school later that my call really did help her cope with it.

Chapter Two

After Shorty's death, mother and my older sister decided they wanted to move down to Loganville where my other two brother's lived as I was working a long way from my house, gone from early morning until late in the afternoon, and without Shorty being there with them, they were afraid to be there alone.

Henry and I had separated for a while, and I moved in the apartment mother had occupied.

Randy, Cindy, and the children moved into the house with me. Sometime later, they separated and Cindy moved in with her mother.

Cindy passed away when Krista and Jamie were approximately 2 and 4 years old. Randy had custody of them prior to then. He was an excellent father, and raised them alone for more than ten years before he and Teri were married.

They spent a lot of time with Henry and me.

When the hospital told Randy that their mother was likely going to pass away during the night, he took the children out to the pool to tell them. He explained that she would sleep in a very pretty bed called a coffin. When Krista saw the coffin, she said she wanted a pretty bed like her mothers.

I remember seeing Cindy's mother holding Jamie at the coffin and telling him she was in Heaven. He asked her if she was coming back. Cindy died from complications of diabetes. I later took Krista to a furniture store and we bought her a beautiful pink day bed that looked like a princess bed.

The children seemed to adjust to their mother's death as well as they could. They were not use to being with her but every other weekend.

Krista started to school right next door to our house. Jamie and I would stand out by the fence and watch for her to come home. A teacher would stay there and watch until she had reached my yard where I was.

I had everything at my house that I could think of that would make them happy. I built a large sandbox under the mimosa tree, had a little swing next to it, and every toy you could imagine that two little kids would like to play with, plus the pool out back.

After a few months, Randy decided he wanted to have a house built in Buford, which would be closer for him to get to work, by the Interstate.

Henry and I had gone back together and we decided to sell our house and move up there also to be able to help him with the children.

They loved their new house. Jamie would tell people it was on a street with a circle. They lived in a cul-de-sac.

While Henry and I were building our house, Krista and Jamie each had their own little hammers. They helped us build the house, so they told everyone.

Before we knew it, Jamie started to school. He had many friends in his neighborhood. Especially a boy next door named Drew, who also had a brother Krista's age named Daniel.

I especially will always give so much thanks to their mother, Krista Miller. She took Jamie to Bible school with them and Jamie was "saved." I will never get his voice out of my mind when he saw me and said, "Grandmother, I was saved today." I was so proud of him, although Randy had them baptized with him when they were very little. It was in a Methodist Church. When they sprinkled Jamie, he took his hands and covered up his head. That got a laugh out of the congregation.

In the meantime after we moved into our new house, my mother came to live with us again as she had become bedridden. My older sister's health was not good, and mother needed more care than she could give her. My older sister moved in with my younger sister, Connie. Krista and Jamie also had a room there with us as they still stayed with us a lot on the weekends and during the summer.

One afternoon while they were with me, we left mother for just a few minutes to run to the grocery store, which was just one mile away. When we returned, I realized I had left the house key inside. I did not know what I was going to do. Mother could not get out of bed to come let us in. Jamie said, "Grandmother, give me your credit card." I did and he immediately opened the door. I asked him where in the world he learned to do that and he said "television."

The night my mother passed away, Krista and Jamie were there. It was Valentine's Day. Jamie was ten years old, but both he and Krista handled being there when she passed away very well. They both ran into their room and started drawing a picture.

Krista drew a very pretty cross and Jamie wrote a letter. In it he said, "My Great Grandmother lived a long and happy life. She is in Heaven now with my mother.

I know I spoiled Krista and Jamie. Donny had put a pool in the backyard for me. The children would swim until midnight during summer when school was out. When they came in and got ready for bed, I put the heating pad on their feet to get them warm. They loved swimming there.

They had friends that came over often to swim with them. The two boys next door to them came over a lot, as well as a boy across the street. They were never without friends there.

Our house was about six miles from Randy's, but after mother passed away, and Donny bought a condominium and moved out of our basement he was renting, we decided it was too much house for us to keep up, so we sold and moved even closer to Randy.

Immediately Jamie made many friends in that subdivision. One especially named Brandon. They would spend the night at each other's house every weekend.

I would go up to Brandon's to pick up Jamie, and he would be standing on the street corner with his black suitcase with a handle. He carried his X-box with him up there in it. I could not pass that corner going out of our subdivision without getting upset and crying. I could actually see him standing there.

In the room I had used, I had many dolls on the shelves above the windows. I moved out of the room to let Jamie and all his friends, and a lot of them, spend the night there as it had a bathroom for them.

I asked them if they wanted me to take the dolls away and they said, "No, they were their maids, and would clean up their room." Never saw that happen though.

Jamie had a computer and he started writing a book called "Walls of Eternal Flame." Once when I took him to a doctor, he told the doctor he was writing a book. The doctor looked at me with a question in his eyes. I told him he was indeed writing one.
Jamie wrote a poem for his class:

Spring
By Jamie Mobley

So special is this time of year
The shinning water makes me cheer
In this lake of shiny blue gold
It almost makes me shed a tear

Leaves so glorious and youthful
The sky so honest and truthful
One must gaze upon its glory
This tranquil place is so soothful

This wonderful time of year
Will not always be with me here
One sorrowful day it must leave
Without a goodbye or a tear

I hope this place lasts forever
This garden of hope and heather
And if it ends some autumn day
I will not forget it ever

Randy and Teri were married in October 2000. Jamie was so happy to have a mother because he was too young when Cindy died to remember her. Of course, they had pictures of their mother.

Randy wanted them to have a vacation to go out of the country and to fly in an airplane, and get a passport. He and Teri took them to Mexico. They enjoyed the plane ride, as well as the vacation.

Randy always made sure they would do things that they would enjoy and remember.

He had enrolled both of them in Karate, as well as him self.

He had a boat and Jamie and Krista became very good at skiing. In the winter time he took them snowboarding. They had very good lives with a lot of activity and love.

In some of Jamie's schoolwork, I found where he had to write his Values. He got 25 out of 25 points, which is a 100 on this paper:

Values are beliefs, or things we hold dear to us in our lives. I value my friends, family, beliefs, school, and religion. My values are special to me as other people's values are to them. Everyone has values.

I developed my values over time. I have always valued friends and family. I value my beliefs. After going to church more often, I realized that I greatly value my religion. I would not ever change my values.

Mill Creek students probably have a value system much like mine. They value their grades, friends, and probably their families. Many of them value religion.

When I have kids, I will teach them values too. I will teach them to value school and church. They will value family. Friends will be valued as well.

Everyone values something. What I value most is family. They are always there if I should need them. They will help when no one else will.

My family is very important to me.

Jamie wrote this when he was 15 years old.

Over the year I've changed a little. I still have my trademark dark sense of humor. I'm about 5'4". I've noticed many things I've done this year that have changed me.

During the year I have showed many strengths of character, but above all there is one I learned that I should trust people and not keep my guard up all the time. I've made some friends that I probably wouldn't have if I hadn't changed.

Some weaknesses of character have shown themselves also. Like I showed a weakness by lowering myself to a level of desperateness by doing stupid things for attention. I don't know why I was desperate for attention. I could have made a better choice.

My best memory during the year was when I had a lot of people clapped for a poem I wrote and presented. I really felt proud. My worst memory of the year was when I was handed a bad math test grade that greatly affected my grade. I was worried about what I was going to do.

I hope to improve my performance and pass with good grades. When I graduate high school I hope to be doing well. I will try my hardest. I want to be headed on to bigger and better things.

Jamie received a score of 95 on this paper.

Chapter Three

I am back to reality now, remembering the last time I was with Jamie. Wednesday I had taken him to the dentist for the last visit of getting his braces off his teeth.

On the way home, I needed to stop at the grocery store to get some chicken. Jamie wanted me to let him go in and get it for me, as my knee was hurting. I wish I had let him go in; I would sure like to know what kind of chicken I would have had for dinner that night.

Jamie was definitely my buddy. He had started confiding things to me, and just talking like an adult with me. I loved both Nikki and Jamie, but I had Jamie for 15 years to bond with, but only 2 ½ years with Nikki.

Every Friday night I would drive him and a group of his friends over to the mall, and Randy would pick them up. Sometimes I had to make two trips to get all of them over to the mall.

Jamie always knew he had transportation for anywhere he needed or wanted to go. He knew I would be there for him. I expressed this to him very often. His friends often joked that my car was Jamie's taxi. In fact, I had planned to print out a poster to put on my window just before I reached them that read "Jamie's Taxi." For the upcoming week-end, but Randy took them that Friday night, so I was going to use it the following week-end, but that never came to pass.

Later that night at the hospital, around 7:30 p.m. a doctor came in and told us it was over. He was definitely brain dead. I was so afraid he was wrong. He did some tests and showed us that he was indeed dead.

It was the hardest thing I think I will ever go through in my life kissing him goodbye and his heart still beating, and them telling me he was dead. They kept the machine on him until they finished with the organs that would donate.

Randy and Teri talked with Donny about burying Jamie next to Nikki. Donny and I had bought some extra lots when she died. Of course, Donny was more than willing to give them the lot next to her.

He died on Tuesday night, but they did not have visitation at the funeral home until Friday night. They had to give them time to get the undamaged organs to donate.

His heart went to a man in Alabama. After a year, he could have contacted Randy and Teri, but they did not hear from him. They did hear from someone who got a kidney.

Jamie's death was the first time I ever saw Henry cry.

The next morning after he died, Henry and I went over to Randy's to clean up the blood while Randy and Teri had gone to the funeral home to make the arrangements. There was blood all over at the entrance of their room. The shooting happened in Randy and Teri's bedroom. We did not want them to have to look at it every time they went in there, although I am sure they felt the pain every day.

175

A Newspaper article in the morning paper:

Gwinnett Daily

Teen shot by accident:

Boy, 15, in critical condition after playing with gun at Buford home. — A 15 —year-old boy was in critical condition Monday evening after being shot in the head while playing with a friend at his home in Buford.

Authorities said the boy and his 14-year-old friend were home from school by themselves on Martin Luther King Day when they somehow got into a storage area where the victim's parents kept several firearms at 3207 Camens Way. While playing with a gun, it accidentally discharged and the 15-year-old was shot in the head, according to Officer Darren Moloney, spokesman for Gwinnett police. Police did not immediately release the names of the victim or his friend.

"No parents were at home when this took place, but everything in the investigation points to it being an accidental shooting." Moloney said.

Investigators did not know if the gun was loaded or unloaded when the boys found it.

The 14-year-old called 911 and the dispatcher advised him to find an adult. He then ran to a female neighbor in Saddlegate subdivision for help. Relatives arrived at the home short time later and then went to be with the victim at Gwinnett Medical Center.

The 14-old-year and his parents were being questioned by police outside the victim's home Monday as crime scene investigators gathered evidence.

Gwinnett Daily

Wounded Mill Creek student dies

A 15-year-old Mill Creek High School student, who was shot in the face while handling a loaded gun Monday, has died, Gwinnett County police said.

Police on Tuesday night could not say when the teen died. He had been in critical condition in the intensive care unit of Gwinnett Medical Center since the shooting Monday.

"Per standard procedure, there will be an autopsy." Officer Darren Moloney said in a statement. "The investigation is still active, and is still being treated as an accidental shooting."

The victim, identified as Jamie Mobley, was at his Buford home with a 14-year-old friend when the shooting occurred. At the time, no adults were in the house, located at 3207 Camens Way, Police said.

Police would not say who was holding the gun when it discharged. They also refused to reveal what kind of gun was involved.

Jamie's parents own several handguns that were locked in a storage area. The teenagers found a way to unlock the storage area and get the gun, Moloney said.

The shooting occurred on the Martin Luther King Jr. holiday, when students are out of school.

Classes at Mill Creek resumed Tuesday with the sobering announcement that Jamie had been critically wounded by gunfire over the weekend.

Principal Jim Markham told students and staff that counselors were available for those who needed to talk about their feelings.

Markham asked students to observe a moment of silence "to reflect in his or her own way...in their thoughts or in their prayers, if that was their inclination to do so," Markham said.

Markham said the school was given very few details but shared what it could with students.

A team of five counselors visited Jamie's classes throughout the day to respond to students' concerns and questions. Jamie's companion that day, who has not been identified also is a freshman at Mill Creek.

This companion was either Casey or Brandon, or both, who were Jamie's best friends.

TWO GONE, TOO SOON

Gwinnett Daily

Teen dies after accidental shooting

Detectives investigating death; few details revealed.

A Buford teen that was accidentally shot in the head earlier this week dies Tuesday.

The 15-year-old boy, whom neighbors identified as Jamie Mobley, died Tuesday evening after spending most of the day in critical condition at Gwinnett Medical Center, said Officer Darren Moloney, spokesman for the Gwinnett County Police Department.

Mobley and his 14-year-old friend were by themselves at Mobley's home Monday afternoon on 3207 Camens Way in Buford when they broke into a storage area where his father kept several guns, police said.

Mobley's parents were at work, but he was out of school for the MLK, Jr. holiday, Moloney said.

While the boys were handling the gun, a shot was fired into Mobley's head. Police on Tuesday were not releasing information about which of the boys was holding the gun when it fired or whether they knew it was loaded, citing the pending investigation as a reason for being tight-lipped.

No one answered the phone at Mobley's home on Tuesday. The next-door neighbor, Krista Miller, said the Mobley's are "a very nice family" and the shooting was an unfortunate accident.

I" think it was just a matter of teenage boys being boys, I guess." Miller said. "From what I understood, the father had the gun locked up, and according to the police, I don't think the father was at fault at all."

Detectives are still investigating the shooting, but it is being treated as accidental. The county medical examiner will perform an autopsy on Mobley's body, Moloney said. The 14-year-old was questioned by police Monday evening, then allowed to return to his parent's home in Buford, Moloney said.

After these articles appeared in the paper, a friend of Randy's, Mr. James Highfill of Suwanee wrote this article to the editor:

Gwinnett Daily

Sensationalism gets in way of real story

I am compelled to write a letter to the editor regarding your Jan. 19 headline that read "Teen dies after accidental shooting. Detectives investigation death; few details revealed." The continuation of the article proclaims "Shooting: Autopsy to be performed."

These headlines seem to imply that this tragic accident had some sort of mysterious of nefarious aspects. I believe the headlines are steeped more in an interest of sensationalism rather than fact and what is normal and customary in police investigations of such an incident. "Few details revealed?" Here are the revealed details. I gleaned from your reviewing your article:

The Buford 15-year-old Buford teen, Jamie Mobley, was accidentally shot in the head and died Tuesday. He spent most of the day in critical condition at Gwinnett Medical Center. Mobley and a 14-year-old friend, by themselves at Mobley's home, broke into a storage area where several guns were stored. Mobley's parents were at work, and Mobley were out of school because of the MLK holiday. The boys were handling a gun, a shot was fired into Mobley's head. The investigation is being treated as an accident. The coroner will perform an autopsy. The 14-year-old friend was questioned by police and released to his parents. The details you cited as being withheld by police were: Who was holding the gun at the time the shot was fired and whether the boys knew the gun was loaded.

As you noted, these two details were not being released by the police, Noting the pending investigation. Therefore, apparently based upon the police not releasing two details, you characterized the police as being "tight-lipped" and bannered the headline with "Few details released." Isn't an autopsy standard procedure in accidents such as this tragedy? You also mention, apparently for effect, that "No one answered the phone at Mobley's home Tuesday." They had just lost their son. As you'll read below, I've known the Mobleys for years and respected their grief and privacy enough not to even attempt to call. The fact is that they never left his bedside at Gwinnett medical Center until after he passed. Did you ever consider that would be where they were?

I've known the Mobley family for years. I met Jamie's dad, Randy, on an ocean scuba diving trip. Since then, I've traveled all over the Florida Keys and the Caribbean diving with Randy. Through knowing Randy, I came to know his family, including Jamie, who I soon found out was an absolute joy to be around. I'm afraid you will not find much with which to sensationalize. But the lack of substance doesn't seem to get in the way now, does it? - James T. Highfill, Suwanee

I do not know which of the articles prompted Mr. Highfill to write his article:

Chapter Four

One of Jamie's best friends, Casey, and his mother were great to help us through this terrible time as well as Brandon and many other friends. The kids from school came over and brought posters they had made for Jamie.

Henry and I lived just across the street where Jamie and Krista went to school. All the people at the school were wonderful. They brought over so much food, as well as friends and my Sunday school class.

Kids were in and out all week bringing things to us.

My next-door neighbors, Sara and Art Stallings were wonderful to us through this.

Jamie loved snowboarding, so I decided I wanted to make his flowers for the funeral like a snowboard. Donny got a friend to make the snowboard out of Styrofoam, and I had a picture of Jamie on his snowboard, so I took all that to the florist and they put it together for me. It was made of red roses and turned out beautiful.

This is a picture taken of Jamie on his last snowboarding trip with Randy, Teri, and Krista.

We started making the preparations for the funeral. Donny went to get his haircut, and when he came out and started to leave, a police officer stopped his van. Seems someone had just tried to rob the grocery store next door. Thank goodness Donny had on a black jacket with no hood, as the "would-be robber" had on a black jacket with a hood. That was all we needed to have to deal with that right now.

Rick, Karen and their family were still here. They stayed in a Motel nearby. Karen always said, "You don't have enough hot water" for us to stay with you. They needed more room than I had to spare.

Friday night came and we all gathered at the funeral home. I do not think I have ever seen as many flowers as there were at his funeral. They were all over his room, and all up and down the hall.

There were so many people there, so many young people from school. They were all so upset and crying hysterically.

They could not all get in there at one time. So many people told me later they talked with me at the funeral home, but I did not remember many of them. I guess I was still in shock. I do remember talking with my dear friend Eleanor.

I felt so bad for Randy and Teri. The long line just never ended of people wanting to extend their sympathy. I knew how tired they must have been getting, but they stayed until the last one talked with them.

They buried Jamie in his new black leather jacket. Randy had taken him shopping on Sunday before the shooting on Monday, and bought him the black leather jacket. He was so proud of it. Randy said he saw him hanging it in his closet that night.

We put so much in Jamie's coffin. He was writing his book, "Walls of Eternal Flame." Randy took it to the printers and had it printed and bound even though it was not finished. He put that in his coffin. Jamie's favorite drink was Vanilla Coke. He had some of those in there. Krista and Randy wrote something in some books and put in his coffin. I wrote him a letter and put in there. They buried his cell phone with him.

185

The kids from school had so many posters with Vanilla Coke cans attached to them.

Jamie's favorite "toy" was a little stuffed cow that came from McDonalds. His friend Casey said that one day they were talking about putting something in his aunt's coffin. He said Jamie made the remark that if he died he would want "cow" put in his coffin. Randy went home, got cow, and put in his coffin.

This little cow went everywhere with Jamie. It went to school with him and the teacher would send notes home about what cow did during the day. Everyone knew Jamie did not go anywhere without cow. It even went to Randy and Teri's wedding in his Tuxedo pocket.

Jamie and Casey made several "movies" about cow. They would get my camcorder and go outside and cow would perform. After Jamie died I was looking at the movies and to my surprise, my Royal Dalton "Old Country Roses" china was out in the yard with cow, and he was drinking out of one of the cups.

Now we all have a Christmas tree with many cows on it.

The next day was the funeral; it was Saturday. There were so many people there that they filled the chapel at the funeral home, and was lined up along the walls, as well as filled the outside of the chapel. The man from the funeral home told me Jamie had broken the record of attendance.

My sister Betty said her husband, Donald, cried all through the funeral.

It was raining during the burial. I just went through the motions as I did at Nikki's funeral. I could not believe I was burying another grandchild. It brought back all the memories of Nikki's funeral just standing there with her grave next to his.

Jamie's birthday was two weeks after Nikki's, and he died just two weeks before she died. Of course, it was 2005 when he died, and 1981 when Nikki died.

The eulogy was beautiful as if any eulogy could be. The pastor asked the young people not to treat the one that shot Jamie bad. That it was an accident.

The one that shot Jamie was at the funeral, and at the burial site. To my knowledge, no one was rude to him.

I could not help but remember a time when I saw him an incident earlier. Jamie was spending the weekend with us as he did so often, and asked me to take him to his house to get something he needed. Going down the road near his house, he saw his friend that shot him, walking down the road. Jamie hid in the floor of my car. I asked him why he was doing that and he said, "(his friend) will kill me if I don't stay here and play with him.

When they lowered Jamie's coffin in the ground, Casey took off his new black leather jacket and spread it over the coffin. I knew Casey loved his jacket as much as Jamie, as that was the trend with kids then. The next week his mother and I took Casey to a store and bought him another black leather jacket.

The funeral home employees were so good to us. They were the same funeral home as Nikki's, except located in Snellville while she was in Lawrenceville. When Nikki died, there was no Snellville funeral home.

They cut several locks of Jamie's hair in the back, tied a ribbon them and gave to us. I have my lock in the frame with Jamie's poem by my bed.

After the funeral, several of my cousins as well as a neighbor had prepared food for everyone to come and eat. I had written directions to my house and had them sent to everyone. A large crowd followed us home. Jackie, a friend I had gone to school with and graduated with, came with us and helped serve and clean up.

Everyone left to go home to his or her every day lives, and left us here to deal with our grief. Isn't that usually the way it goes?

Several weeks later, I went to a grief class at my church. I came home as much upset as when I left. It was to last one hour. One of the people took up most of the class talking about her grief.

It seems she had a brother that lived down the street from her and she was so upset when he died because she did not know about his illness. She had not seen him in nine months. It seemed to me if she cared much about him, she would have visited him during the nine months, and she would have known he was sick. It just seemed like her grief was a marble compared to my bowling ball.

When they turned to me, I told them lets just see the movie they were going to show when we finished talking. I knew I would need more than just the few minutes left to talk about my grief.

I did not feel like going anywhere or seeing anyone. I dropped out of the Garden Club where I was secretary. There just did not seem there would ever be any happiness in my future.

One relative told me I had to just get over it and get on with my life. How can you just make one get on with her life? It has to come natural. Everyone grieves in different ways. I read all the books I could find about handling grief. They all said the same. It just takes time and prayer.

We all wanted to know what Jamie's thoughts were his last day and what he said. Randy wrote a letter to the young boy that shot Jamie, just to ask these questions. He did not reply.

Chapter Five

The principal of the school called Randy and Teri and told them they were going to have a ceremony at the school and retire Jamie's locker. They also said the Atlanta Journal and Constitution paper would be there to carry the story.

When we got there, they decorated Jamie's locker. Randy and Teri had taken Jamie's book bag with some of his personal belongings and tennis shoes and placed in the locker.

The principal said the locker would stay locked forever and never to be opened again. He said in years to come, the students might not know who Jamie Mobley was, but they would know he was someone special.

Jamie was the first to die as a student while attending the school since it opened. A couple of years later, there was another student killed.

Jamie's pastors from his church attended the ceremony. It was one time we had prayer in school.

They also said they were going to place a bench at the school in memory of Jamie. Again, my good friends Nita Holt and Bonnie contributed to the cost of the bench, as well as

Jamie's church. Nita and Bonnie are always there for me in time of need.

On each occasion at the school, they decorated Jamie's locker to the hilt. On the anniversary of his death, his birthday, Valentine's Day, and every other time they saw fit. The kids would call me and ask me to come over to the school to see his locker, which I did as I just lived across the street.

A newspaper article:

Gwinnett Daily

A pair of black Converse sneakers with dirt still on the soles. A can of Vanilla Coke. A backpack stuffed with a sweatshirt and 50 pages of an unfinished manuscript. Sealed in a locker. Forever.

It's the way Mill Creek High School in Gwinnett County remembers family. Jamie Mobley was one of them - a 15-year-old freshman finding his way around school in Mill Creek's inaugural year.

He was a kid quick with a joke and even quicker to bum a dollar for a soda, friends say.

He wanted to be a writer.

On Tuesday, Mill Creek High School principal Jim Markham stood before a huddle of Jamie's sobbing relatives and friends to preside over a unique memorial. He ordered Jamie's locker permanently sealed.

"We are creating a memorial to a student to remind everybody who walks through these halls

of the sanctity of life." Markham told the crowd of 60. "We are going to retire his locker forever." The announcement was met with sniffles. Jamie's parents, Teri and Randy Mobley stepped forward to place artifacts in the locker. His sister, Krista, 17, a Mill Creek student, cried uncontrollably. Jamie's paternal grandparents and friends held hands.

The memorial was Markham's way of helping a new school cope with the death of a student. Jamie died on January 18, 2005, after he was accidentally shot in the head.

Across Georgia and the nation, public schools pay tribute to deceased students and faculty in a variety of ways. Some schools plant trees. Some add memorial benches. Others celebrate lost lives with a yearbook page. Some create memorial scholarships.

Tucker High School in DeKalb County dedicated its school gym earlier this month in the memory of Coach William S. Venable, who was gunned down with his son in a home invasion in January 2004.

Elsewhere in the district, a memorial park was erected near Dunwoody High School to honor Louie Nava, a student murdered in 1998.

In Gwinnett, a mural in the new Norton Elementary School gym bears a portrait of a third-grader in a baseball cap that drowned last school year.

At Mill Creek, a plaque reads: "This locker has been retired in the memory of Jamie Mobley."

Shortly after the school bell rang, dozens of students in the school passed through the hall. Some students walked by the locker without noticing. Others came by to touch it and snap pictures.

"Nice, for shizzle (sure) said one student.

"We miss you, Jaaaamie," yelled another.

The memorial is a fitting tribute to a freshman who was always the center of a crowd, said Brendan Prickett, a close friend of Jamie's. "He made you laugh. Life is a lot harder without Jamie. I think about him everyday.

NICK ARROYO / Staff

194

TWO GONE, TOO SOON

An article in the school paper:

Hard to Say Goodbye

When Mill Creek High School lost one of its very own in January, students showed enormous support and mournful sorrow. Jamie Mobley, a freshman at MCHS, passed away after a tragic gun accident at his home in Buford. The incident occurred on Monday, January 17th — on the Martin Luther King Jr. holiday of " MLK day." Jamie was shot in the head with a pistol and passed away the next day, Darren Mooney, labeled the incident an accidental shooting. Mobley passed away at Gwinnett Medical Center on January 18, 2005 — leaving behind his mother, father, and sister, Krista, who is a junior at MCHS.

"Jamie was an awesome writer" said MCHS freshman Josh Stowe. "He wrote a bunch of songs for our band that were so good. I'm gonna miss him because of his kindness. Jamie was definitely one of the nicest kids I knew, even though he didn't say much," Josh continued. Many students have also expressed their feelings about Jamie, writing notes on the poster outside of his locker. Heart-rending comments like "We love you Jamie" and "We will never forget you" are commonplace comments on the posters outside of the late freshman's locker.

The Mill Creek Student body will forever remember this loss of life in its inaugural year. The reaction of the freshman class, the school, and

195

the community to the tragedy was commendable. Along with the rest of Mill creek High School, we wish the best for Jamie's loved ones in the coming years.

Also, there was a picture of Jamie along with a picture of some of the posters on his locker.

I took Jamie's school picture over to FedEx Kinko's to have it enlarged and put on a 14 x 17 poster in a frame. When I returned to pick it up, he gave this letter me:

Mrs. Short, I have been following the tragic loss of your Grandson, Jamie, on the news and wanted to give you our sincere condolences for your family's loss. I cannot begin to imagine what your family must be going through; however, as a small gesture of kindness, we would like to donate these pictures to your family on the behalf of the coworkers of the Buford FedEx Kinko's location.

Sincerely, Greg Matthews, Manager

That touched my heart so very much. They did such a beautiful job with the picture. I think almost all of his friends, as well as family went over to have one made for themselves.

So many people did such wonderful things for us. Dianne, Casey's mother came over and planted a memory garden for Jamie in my backyard. She filled it full of roses, and many other flowers. It was just beautiful.

Dianne Fisher planting the memory garden in my backyard. She filled it full of knock out roses, a little buggy with a little boy sitting in it, other statues, and many, many other plants. It was the most beautiful memory garden one can imagine.

Some of the emails that came over the computer:

JAMIE I LOOVE YOU SOOOOOOOOOO MUCH... WATCH OVER EVERY1 AND IL SEE YOU SOMETIME IN THE FUTURE...AND IM SRY FOR ALL THE CRAP I GIVE YOU HANNAH

Yeah, and im sorry that I annoyed the hell outta him all the time...hehe.but I hope he forgives me for it — Dani

WE MISS U JAMIE !!!!!!!!!!!!!!!!!!!!!!!!!!!!!!!!!!!!!!!

Hey Jamie I miss you so much. I just wanted to tell you I love you and miss you. I guess I will see you tonight. Love Chelsea

I LOVE U !!!!!!!!! UR THE BEST MONGOOSE EVER!!

Watch over us from heaven…yoo ish living forever, and I will see u one day n so will Chelsea and we will give u a big bear hug!!!

I still talk to yoo a lot, so…don't ignore me…and u kno, it wouldn't hurt to say sumin bak….lol

Buhbyes…c u.tomorrow

I love you sooooooo much I hope you know that piz if you can talk back to us just plz say something to help us all from up in heaven.

Hey Jamie!!! Hope ur watching us all from heaven and I want u to kno there's always a place for u in my heart!! I love you!!! Alyssa

Jamie, please watch over us all! You are missed by soooooooo many people that's it's not even funny. We all love you Jamie, and we still talk to you. Please respond Jamie…. Brittany

Hey Jamie!! Hope ur watching over us!!

Jamie...im sorry I missed you...my mom was being a meanie...im just so curious what it's like up there...in heaven... ILL BE THE BEST MONGOOSE I CAN UNTIL I SEE YOU AGAIN!! We love you soooooo much Courtney Boland

Jamie!!! Just comin to say I love you again....

Yeh, plz answer us back...plz....

gave u another doller today....

I miss you so much...me and Chelsea left you a message on ur cell, cuz we kno u have it...so don't ferget to check ur messages an call us back....

We love you more and more each day...and it hurts that we cant see you smile except in pictures and dreams for a long time...and I cant chase u around for hugs for a while either... and the closest we can get to you, is 6 feet away...except in spirit, which I ho-e is standing over my shoulder as I type this rite now....

We r goin to hav a bunch of memorials for u...and...parties and stuff...ill visit you soon Jamie much love

can't hardly wait til I get to see you again, babe...and gosh, if I never sed this before...ur relly cute...*wink wink*

I love u tons n tons ntons....*Dani*

Jamie dude ill miss u man.u were one of the coolest kids I know…send us a sign so we know ur happy up there, we miss u lots

Don't forget about the gummy worms! I miss you Alissa

We miss you Jamie. We all love you so much, keep watching over us, hope you're likin' haven. Love always, Grit

we love you so much, hope you are rockin out on all the harps. Lol

JAMIE I LOOVE YOU SOOOOOOOMUCH…WATCH OVER EVERY1 AND IL SEE YOU SOMETIME IN THE FUTURE…AND IM SRY FOR ALL THE CRAP I GIVE YOU

These are just a few of the many, many e-mails that came over Jamie's computer.

Everyone had a very hard time after Jamie's death. I know I could not go anywhere, and did not want to. I did try to go to church, but always got upset when I saw some boys Jamie's age and started crying in church.

Krista especially had a hard time. Every time the 18th of a month came around, she would get extremely upset and the school counselor would call me to come get her. It was the 18th when he died. Krista had always been Jamie's "little mother." Growing up they had always been by each other's side.

On one evening, I got word from Randy and Teri's church that there was going to be a candlelight vigil in their yard that night.

We went over there just before dark. I could not believe the beautiful sight I saw coming up the road. There must have been a hundred people walking up the road with a lit candle in their hand. They had parked their cars down the road to surprise Randy and Teri.

Several of Jamie's teachers were there that night. They had many nice things to say about Jamie.

That was the first time I had heard Randy pray since he was small and asked the blessing before a meal.

After Henry, a neighbor and I, had finished cleaning up the blood from the shooting, Randy and Teri had the carpet replaced. They saved the carpet and planned to take it to the lake on Memorial Day when they had their annual camping outing. Jamie had always gone with them to the lake. They burned the carpet in a bonfire in memory of Jamie. They also took the gun that killed Jamie and threw it in the deepest part of the lake.

After about a year Randy and Teri decided they could no longer live in the house because of too many memories. Everyone told them to wait at least a year before making any decisions, which they did.

Henry and I went over every day and helped get the house in order to sell. Henry did all the necessary repairs, and I did the painting.

When I got to Jamie's room, it was so hard to paint it.

Every time when the school bus came in the afternoon, I got very upset. I kept looking for Jamie to get off the bus and he did not. Once I went out back and sat on the steps and cried. Jamie's boxer "Rocky" came up and sat beside the fence as though he knew why I was crying.

After just a short while, Randy and Teri got a contract on the house.

They planned to move to Covington and build on her land next to her parents. After they moved, Henry and I decided to sell our house, as there was no family close to us up in the Buford area.

We got our house ready to put on the market. Henry had to have a leg by-pass, so I packed everything in our house by myself. We got a contract on our house while he was in the hospital, but before we could move, I had to have knee surgery.

I was glad to be selling our house. I could hardly go into the room Jamie shared with so many of his friends. It was just too painful for me to stay there. Every time I tried to vacuum the floor, I could literally see Jamie lying there in his sleeping bag.

We moved just a few weeks after my surgery. Henry was still on crutches and I was on crutches. The boys came and loaded the boxes, and we had movers come for the furniture. Rick, Karen, and children came over from Alabama and helped load things into Randy's trailer. We went through Christmas without a tree for the first time ever.

In the caravan while we were moving, I was in the last car to follow. I kept lagging behind and Randy called me on the cell phone to see where I was.

I just could not go any faster, I felt as though I was leaving someone behind.

Chapter Seven

We all finally settled into our different houses. We so often mentioned, "what would Jamie think?" or "would Jamie like this?" Jamie's friends still kept in touch with us and called often.

Once when we went to the cemetery there were Vanilla Cokes lined all the way around Jamie's grave.

Randy and Teri rented a house in Covington until they could build a house. Within a few months after they settled there, Teri lost her mother to Kidney failure. That was such a blow to her.

I have to keep Jamie's picture where I could see him everyday. I put his over the mantel in our kitchen, and put Nikki's over the mantel in our living room. I see him watching me every day.

Krista had graduated just before we all moved from the Buford area. Randy and Teri received a letter from Jamie and Krista's school when it came time for the graduation in which Jamie would have been. They were going to give him an honorary diploma.

Randy and Teri had paid a deposit, which was non-refundable for a cruise and could not attend the ceremony the school had planned for Jamie.

Henry, Krista, and I went to the graduation. They had us reserved parking, and reserved seats. They definitely treated us as VIP as shown on our reserved seats.

When we received the announcement with all the graduating students listed, we noticed Jamie's name was among them.

Also, at the top was:

Mill Creek High School Class of 2008

We, the class of 2008, have called ourselves the "Cornerstone Class" because we are the first four year class to graduate from Mill Creek High School. We would like to take this time to thank the administration, faculty, and parents for their support over the past four years. **We would also like to dedicate this ceremony to the memory of James Randall Mobley and John Michael Sefcik.** Michael lost his life after Jamie.

We were so very touched. We wondered what they would do when they got to Jamie's name. There were many hundred students graduating.

When they got to his name, the speaker said, "Would everyone take a moment of silence as we look to the marquee and remember Jamie Mobley?"

There was a huge picture of Jamie. I just came unglued!

For a minute there was complete silence. No one made a sound except for Krista and me crying. It was amazing.

After the ceremony, the principal came up to us and presented to Krista a diploma with Jamie's name just like everyone else's, and a bouquet of red roses.

That school had just done such wonderful things for our family that we will never forget.

They dedicated a page in the yearbook to Jamie. It read:

> *"In loving memory of Jamie Mobley, 1989 — 2005. As we celebrate the joys we've shared our first year here at Mill Creek High School, we should also remember our first sorrows. The yearbook staff extends our sympathy to the family and friends of Jamie Mobley, who was tragically taken from us this January.*

This was another sad time for us, as we knew Jamie would have enjoyed having all his friends sign his yearbook. Randy had the ones he knew sign the book.

It was not too much longer after Teri lost her mother until Teri lost her father. They did not have to build a house as they inherited her father's beautiful house.

We knew how much Jamie would have loved living out there with horses, and having 65 acres to explore. Krista had a job and lived in another area.

She had often mentioned that she did not like being "an only child," after Jamie's death.

In 2009, Randy and Teri adopted a beautiful baby girl. Krista just loves Cassie to death. Now Krista will no longer be an only child.

My Author Bio

I was born in Gwinnett County, Georgia in 1937. I have three sons and 13 grandchildren here on earth, and 3 in Heaven. My love for my children prompted me to write this book as all three of my sons have lost a child. One murdered, one stillborn, and one shot by a friend. My Faith has brought me through many, many tragedies in my life, as my book describes.

I started writing this book after my granddaughter's murder in 1981. I was hospitalized twice due to getting so upset while writing, and stopped writing for a while.

I am now 73 years old and was afraid if I didn't write it now, I never would. I want my grandchildren, and future grandchildren, to know about their cousins, and my love for all my children, and to know there are not enough words in the dictionary to describe my love for them.

Would you like to see your manuscript become a book?

If you are interested in becoming a PublishAmerica author, please submit your manuscript for possible publication to us at:

acquisitions@publishamerica.com

You may also mail in your manuscript to:

**PublishAmerica
PO Box 151
Frederick, MD 21705**

www.publishamerica.com

LaVergne, TN USA
09 March 2011
219341LV00001B/44/P